WINNING
IS EVERYTHING

Dr. Tony Hart,
WINNING
IS EVERYTHING
Forward by Tony Evans

WINNING IS EVERYTHING
By: Tony Hart
Copyright © 2010
GOSPEL FOLIO PRESS
All Rights Reserved

Published by
GOSPEL FOLIO PRESS
304 Killaly St. W.
Port Colborne, ON L3K 6A6
CANADA

ISBN: 9781897117750

Cover design by Lisa Martin

All Scripture quotations from the
King James Version unless otherwise noted.

Printed in USA

Dedication

This book is dedicated to my Lord and Saviour Jesus Christ who won the greatest victory of all.

Acknowledgements

Winning Is Everything represents one of the goals that I have had since entering the ministry several years ago. As with several other accomplishments, I owe a great indebtedness to so many people who have helped in countless ways. Thanks to the entire Montco Bible Fellowship family which has inspired and supported me through all my formal school work as well as allowing me study time where many of the thoughts presented in this book were developed. My church family represents for me the grace of God to whom I owe everything.

Thanks to Lynda Liverpool, my secretary, who spent many hours transcribing and typing. I also want to thank Garth Wright who did the final editing and rewrote many of my sentences. Without his help this book would not have been completed. He guided me through a process that I was totally unfamiliar with. I will never forget his effort at a time of trial in his own life.

I also want to thank my parents, Dr. B. Sam Hart and Joyce Hart. They have been winners indeed. I thank them for providing the family in which I grew up and being the kind of mentor in the ministry that has supplied much wisdom over the years.

Last, but not least, I want to acknowledge the support and help that Carol, my wife, has been to me in my ministry. I would not be who I am without her much less the author of this book.

Foreword

Every year in January, the two of the best football teams from two American cities face off at the Super Bowl. One usually walks away experiencing the thrill of victory and the other the agony of defeat. In one city, there is a parade and celebration, in the other there is usually frustration, disappointment and defeat. Both teams took the field, only one was victorious.

What is true in the Super Bowl is often true in the Christian life. As a pastor I have witnessed many Christians who move from one problem to another, perpetually living in the agony of defeat. On the other hand I have also observed Christians who face the same problems of the defeated Christian, but somehow find ways to make the opposition fumble and come up with big plays necessary to be winners.

What is the difference? Those who are victorious don't let the opposition throw them off their game plan. They prepare hard by studying the enemy and focusing intensely on executing God's plan even in the midst of conflict. Defeated Christians, however, allow the circumstances to redefine their strategy.

That's what excites me about *Winning Is Everything*. Tony Hart addresses the issue of the victorious Christian life. Using the book of Numbers from the Old Testament as the foundation for his exposition, Tony reveals how the spiritual victories received by the saints of old can be ours today. He shows us how God desires to lead us, provide for us, protect us, and strengthen us in the midst of various situations.

With contemporary illustrations, clear Biblical exposition and in the common man's language, Tony helps us to experientially know what it means to be more than conquerors in Christ, and how we can more seriously accept our responsibility to remain faithful to God's Word, while courageously preventing the enemy's plan from governing our lives.

May God richly bless you as you read and apply these practical truths from God's Word.

Dr. Tony Evans
Senior Pastor – Oak Cliff Bible Fellowship
President – Urban Alternative.

Table of Contents

1. The Strategy 13
2. God Goes Before Us 25
3. Keep Your Hands Up 39
4. God Leads In Every Situation 49
5. Follow The Cloud 59
6. The Trumpets Signal What Time It Is 69
7. God Is In The Drivers Seat 79
8. Bear Up Under The Pressure 93
9. Show Me The Ransom 105
10. Spy For What? 117

1
The Strategy

The story goes that a mild-mannered man was sitting at a bar located on the top floor of a high-rise in Manhattan. He was calmly throwing down shots of tequila. An observer at the other end of the bar watched in shock as the mild-mannered man downed shot after shot and all of a sudden got up, walked out to the balcony, and jumped off!

A few minutes later the elevator doors opened and there was the mild-mannered man in perfect health! He walked back into the bar, sat down in his seat, and resumed downing more shots of tequila. The observer at the end of the bar was amazed and asked, "How in the world did you pull that off?" The mild-mannered man calmly responded, "The secret is in the tequila. The more tequila you drink the more buoyant you become. When you jump off the balcony you slow down as you approach the sidewalk and come to a nice, soft landing."

The observer wasn't too sure about that, but the mild-mannered man quickly added, "It's true; just look at me. Not a scratch. Now it's your turn." The man at the end of the bar began throwing down shots of tequila, walked out onto the balcony, gave a little salute and jumped off. At the same moment the mild-mannered man raced across the room and jumped off the balcony after him!

A few minutes later the elevator doors opened and the mild-mannered man walked back into the bar with his arm over the shoulder of the now dazed and staggered observer. They walked up to the bar and the bartender said, "Y'know Superman, one of these days you're not gonna beat the guy to the sidewalk."

Clark Kent had a strategy for his little practical joke and he trusted in his super powers in order to be successful. There is a strategy employed against you, against me, and against every Bible believer, but it's not a joke. It's deadly serious and it's being carried out by evil spiritual powers. They are at a chalkboard in the heavens creating a plan to defeat us. If we are going to experience any victory in this life, we need to come up with a counter-strategy and some powerful spiritual armor.

Ephesians chapter six gives us that strategy. It tells us how we need to think and what our perception needs to be to enable us to walk in victory. I'm not going to go into a Biblical exposition of the armour of God, but there are principles in this passage that can help us in our daily lives.

Your Position In Christ

Here is an encouragement from Ephesians 6:10: *"Finally my brethren, be strong in the Lord and in the power of his might."* The first thing to note is that God's strategy for dealing with the enemy requires that you have an appreciation of your position in Christ. When you understand who you are in Jesus Christ and what it means to be a child of God, you will understand that Christ represents all the power, all the strength, and all the enablement you need to walk victoriously in this life.

On one occasion, I spent all day in a seminar for volunteers working at the county prison for Prison Fellowship, a Christian ministry to inmates. As we opened up the seminar, one of the volunteers asked the chaplain of the prison, "Chaplain, why don't you sing a song for us?" The Chaplain's response was, "Well, it's true that through Christ I can do almost all things, but it doesn't include singing!"

Maybe we cannot do all things, but the Bible tells me that through Christ we can do all that Christ leads us to do. To put it another way, all things that we are called to do He enables us to do. People talk about having self-esteem but what we need is a fresh view of who we are in Christ. As believers in Jesus Christ, we're not the ones who should be walking around with our heads hung down, moping around and just barely getting

THE STRATEGY

by. In Him we are enabled; we have strength; we have power.

Some Christians complain, "Oh, the burdens of life are so heavy, I can hardly make it through another day." Paul writes of Christ in Philippians 4:13: *"I can do everything through Him who gives me strength."* It doesn't mean that life is going to be a magic carpet ride. It doesn't mean that we're always going to have an easy time. It doesn't mean that there aren't going to be struggles, or tears, or tragedy. But what it does mean is that through it all Jesus Christ enables us, strengthens us, and allows us to walk in victory.

J. B. Phillips paraphrases Ephesians 1:19-20 this way, "How tremendous is the power available to us who believe in God. When we make firm our connection with God, His life and power flow through us." When we connect ourselves to Jesus Christ, when we get in Christ and when we are found in Him, we have all the power and strength we need to make it through whatever the circumstance may be.

During World War II some of the harbours in Africa were blocked, preventing the Allied ships from getting into the harbour. The Axis forces had dropped huge barges in the water that got stuck in the sand and the big ships couldn't get into the harbours that were critical to the Allied forces. So the military minds got together and came up with an ingenious way to get the barges out of the sand. They took some big oil refinery tanks and filled them with air. Then, when the tide was low, they strapped the tanks to the barges. When the tide rose the tanks pulled up the barges, freed them from the sand and they easily moved the barges out of the harbour.

That seems like a simple solution, but when you stop and think of it, you realize there was a lot going on to make it happen. The power that was focused and harnessed to pull the barges up out of the sand was the result of a rising tide that came from the gravitational pull of the moon, which resulted from the moon's rotation around the earth and the earth's rotation in the solar system that is rotating around the sun.

In the same way, when Jesus Christ is in your life you have all the power of the universe focused to help you through whatever the circumstance you might be facing in your life. All the power in the universe, all the power that keeps the planets in line and all the power in everything that exists on this earth is focused and found in Jesus Christ. He makes that power available to you and me when we're found in Him. You see; we're His children, His spiritual children. As His beloved children He's not going to leave us stuck in the sand. Right now it might seem as though there's no hope for you in your present circumstances, but simply understanding your position in Christ puts you on the winning side.

Part of the strategy for living a victorious life is an appreciation of your position in Christ. Understand that the King of kings, the Lord of lords, loves and cares about you. He cares so much that He gave His life for you and made it possible for you to benefit from a wonderful position in Christ with all of the power that this position brings to us.

Withstanding the Devil

Ephesians 6:11 encourages us to, "Put on the whole armor of God that you may be able to stand against the wiles of the devil." It's a strategy that requires an appreciation of the opposition that we face as it goes on to say in verse 12: *"For we do not wrestle against flesh and blood, but against principalities, against powers, against the rulers of the darkness of this age, against spiritual hosts of wickedness in the heavenly places."*

Since there is an ongoing strategy session with the principalities and powers in the heavens working to defeat us it is no accident that sometimes we lose our faith. It is no accident that circumstances come into your life that test your faith in God and it's no accident that sometimes you wonder, "Where is God, anyway?" It is no accident because there is a deliberate strategy against you.

This is an area that is difficult to talk about. Just walk down the street and start telling people about the devil. They might call the police and have you put in a straitjacket and thrown in a rubber room somewhere. People don't want to hear about the devil because it's like a fairytale to them. But tell them about some spiritualist or a séance and many people will be into it. Spiritualism is one of the best-sellers in bookstores now. Every-

THE STRATEGY

body's fascinated by ESP, TM, and New Age philosophy—but once you start talking about Biblical realities they think what you are saying is ludicrous.

As Christians we need to be aware of the skeptical nature of the world around us that the spiritual forces will try to use to influence our way of thinking. If we are going to live a victorious life, we need to stand up for, as well as appreciate, who we are in Christ and respect the fact that the opposition has the power to affect our lives.

I remember reading a story about a Sunday school leader who was teaching the children in church a song with the words, "He has conquered every foe." Of course, the kids were a little puzzled so the leader had to explain to them, "A foe is like an enemy and our enemy begins with the letter 'd'." He was thinking about the devil. One little hand went up and the boy said, "Oh, you mean the Democrats!"

Well, I guess the politics of that family came right out on the table! But the Democrats are not the enemy. The Republicans are not the enemy and neither is the Reformed Party. It's not your boss or your irritable neighbor. And that spouse of yours is not the enemy. They are not the problem! Your problem is not the people around you or the situations that you face. The enemy, the opposition, the person who wants you to fall is the devil himself. We are engaged in spiritual warfare that's being waged in heavenly places. It's a battle that's taking place beyond our sphere of knowledge and beyond our consciousness. It's a battle that is way over our heads but it's being waged against us.

One of my favorite coaches, Buddy Ryan said, "You've got to know offense in order to coach defense." It's true with the Christian life as well. We have to have a handle on the opposition in order to strategize, defeat, and walk successfully against the opposition. You've got to understand who he is and how he operates.

Let me tell you a little about the devil. First of all, he's cunning, he's deceitful and he lies. He's the father of lies. On the other hand, he looks good. He's handsome, he's cute, he's sexy and sometimes he appears as the angel of light. He's alluring and promises pleasure. He hands hold out bait that you will want to reach out for. That's why as believers we can't play with the devil because he's dangerous. Don't date his representatives. Stay as far away from him as you can. Don't listen to his lies or underestimate the cunning deception of this spiritual enemy. Keep yourself embedded in the Word of God and keep your mind focused on what God's truth is. By doing this you won't let Satan divert you with any of his lies.

The "Evil Day"

Look at Ephesians 6:13: *"Therefore, take up the whole armor of God, that you may be able to withstand in the evil day and having done all, to stand."* The strategy requires not only an appreciation of who we are in Christ and the opposition, but it must also include an appreciation of the evil day—the day and times in which we live. I would like to challenge you today that just because your credit card is paid down, just because you have a paycheck coming in every Friday and you're able to make that rent or mortgage payment, does not mean that we are not living in the evil day.

When we find ourselves with the bills paid and our health is pretty good, all of a sudden we put our Bibles down and we don't have time for prayer any more. Everything is looking good, the retirement plan is building up, we're able to save some money, we're making progress through life, we're moving up the social ladder, and we get duped into thinking that we're not in the evil day. But these days in which we live are what the Bible describes as the evil day. It's only when some madman crashes a commercial airliner into a skyscraper that we wake up and understand how bad things are and dust off our Bibles, grab our devotionals and search out God in prayer.

Even when we don't see the evil going on and we're not in immediate trouble, even when everything is going fine, we need to appreciate the fact that our lives are lived in the context of the evil day. You don't have to go much further than the news to figure it out. We live in a time when a multimillionaire sports star murders his pregnant girlfriend and people end up chuckling about it over the water cooler at the office. We've become so hardened by the insane crimes that we can see everyday on the evening news that they become a joke to us!

THE STRATEGY

We live in evil times when a recent President of the United States seemed to live by the song, "Love the One You're With," carrying on an extramarital affair in his office. I don't care how many times your stock splits, what kind of car is parked in your driveway or how many square feet you have in your house; when your kids have to go through a metal detector to gain entrance to high school, these are evil days. In the past 30-year period, there was a 560% increase in illegitimate births. Schools educate our kids about birth control and offer classes in sex education, but all the while the rate of illegitimate births and sexually transmitted diseases is skyrocketing. This is clearly what the Bible calls "the evil day".

During this same 30-year period, when Americans have more money than ever, there's a 400% increase in the divorce rate and a 200% increase in teenage suicide. These aren't statistics made up of only non-Christian, ungodly families. This includes the Christians! Satan is having a heyday in our churches, destroying our leaders, our marriages and our families without a lot of opposition. He's ripping out from under us the foundation of our society!

I spoke at a banquet for a church in Philadelphia that was celebrating its 40th anniversary. One of the missionaries the church supports was there and shared that during the past year, while they were giving their lives to God on the mission field, their 16-year old son committed suicide. Don't get duped by the media or the world's definition of success to think anything else—we live in evil days.

Satan wants to blind us to how bad things are because he knows that you won't fight as long as you think that everything is okay. As long as you're passive and just take a ride through life, Satan will win. Our strategy needs to include the knowledge that we have the power in Christ to change things, an appreciation for who the enemy is, and that our lives are lived in the context of evil days.

Standing Against the Devil

"Therefore, take up the whole armor of God, that you may be able to withstand in the evil day and having done all, to stand." (Eph.

6:13) Our strategy must also require an appreciation of the goals and there are two mentioned in this verse. First of all, the Apostle Paul talks about withstanding, and secondly he talks about standing. The goal, to *"withstand in the evil day,"* is a defensive goal. Sometimes all you can do is to stand defensively against the onslaughts and fiery darts of the devil. There are times when the fiery darts are flying at us and the pressures of life come down upon us in such a way that all you can do is stand in a defensive posture. But God gives us the power to be able to withstand even in this evil day. Christians should not be the ones who are falling back, backsliding and throwing our hands in the air. We have the power to withstand.

There are times in all of our lives when the pressures are so severe that our first goal is simply to hold on for another day, or to grab our Bible and say, "Lord, help! I need you and I love you and I need you to speak to my heart right now." Even when you don't see how it's going to work out and you don't understand how God's going to pull you through, in faith you are able to turn to Him and say, "Lord, help me to withstand in this evil day."

But if withstanding is defensive, standing is offensive. Standing against the devil and his world system is an offensive orientation and that needs to be our goal. It's offensive because we are to effect change. That's why Jesus said we are like salt and light. Salt has a preservative effect on the meat that it's put on and light has an effect on the darkness that it's placed in. Christians bring a message that preserves life and brings light to a world struggling in darkness. We are the ones who need to cultivate an offensive stand against the devil in our communities, in our schools and in our churches.

Christians Need To Get Involved

The Church and God's people need to stand up against the devil and his program. Why are so many Christians too busy to make it to PTA and school board meetings when critical decisions are being made in our schools? We need to stand at those meetings. We need to be at the city council meetings when important issues are being debated and decided, and we need to

THE STRATEGY

speak up about that which is on God's heart. We also need to be on the lookout for the devil in our churches. He wants to deceive the church and replace God's program with his own.

We need to be standing against the devil in our families! That means guarding against the influences that find their way into our home. It also means providing the discipline that will prevent giving Satan the opportunity to come against a member of our family. In order to experience victory in the evil day, we need to take a stand against the devil, in our family and in our home, and make our stand known.

Paul expresses this goal for himself beautifully. In Ephesians 6:19 he writes, *"And pray for me, that utterance may be given to me, that I may open my mouth boldly to make known the mystery of the Gospel."* Paul is saying, "Look, my goal is to stand, to have God give me the power to speak and to speak boldly and make the Gospel known to the people." This is exactly the job that was given to the Church in Ephesians chapter three. It's our job, and should be our goal, to stand up in the face of the devil in an offensive fashion, to make known the mystery of the gospel and to let people know that Jesus loves them.

Now the question is, "How do we do that?" There are some people who think the best way is to stand out on the corner and hand out tracts. Certainly, there are testimonies of people who have been saved and brought to Jesus Christ because somebody handed them a tract that had the Gospel message in it. Their hearts were ready to receive it, they read it, they bowed their hearts and they established a relationship with God.

However, as each year goes by, less and less of that kind of evangelism can be done because we don't live in a Christian country anymore. Wake up and smell the coffee! We don't even live in a Bible-literate country anymore. The vast majority of kids today don't know Moses from Paul. We can't go on the assumptions that we used back in the 50's because they're not true anymore. The average person no longer accepts that this Bible is God's Word. You've got to demonstrate that to them.

The average person is not willing to buy your message simply because you tell them that Jesus loves them. Their ears are closed and they're not about to listen. You might know Jesus love because He has done something in your life. You might understand it because you've experienced it. But for many others out there for whom God is a distant, historical or theoretical figure, they're just not going to swallow it. They don't live in a world where a biblical worldview is accepted.

Love Them Into the Kingdom

As we get further into this new millennium, increasingly the job of doing ministry and evangelism has to be based on love and sharing love. Joe Aldridge makes the argument in his book, *Friendship Evangelism,* that we need to show love to people and love them until they ask, "Why are you doing this for me?" That's the perfect opportunity to share with them what God has done for you.

One of the stories Aldridge tells in his book is about a missionary at a supermarket. When she got to the register there was a poor woman in front of her. You've seen those people at the supermarket (maybe you've been there yourself) when they don't have enough money and they have to start taking stuff back to lower the total. The poor woman said, "Well, I don't need the soda, and I don't need the popcorn." But then the missionary noticed that the woman needed to get her bill down even lower and she was starting to put back necessities like milk and bread.

The missionary's heart went out to this woman and she told the woman she could put back some of the essential things. She said to her, "I'll pay the difference for that." Afterwards, the poor woman waited for her outside of the supermarket until she paid for her own groceries and asked her, "You don't know me. Why would you do that for me?" That's right out of the book of love evangelism. It's a classic case. If you show God's love to somebody, what's going to happen? They're going to ask (because we live in such a cold world where everybody has their own agenda), "Why would you love me that way?" And when somebody asks you why you're motivated to care it's the perfect opportunity to share with that person the love of God. Love them until they ask you, "Why?"

Be Bold For Christ

Paul tells us that we need to put ourselves in a position where we can speak boldly, where we can make known the mystery of the Gospel. Whether you do it to a neighbor, a co-worker or even to a stranger, it happens best when you go out of your way to love them so unconditionally that they think you are absolutely crazy. And guess what? They might even take advantage of you for a while. But when you keep on loving them they will not only realize that you're not crazy, but sooner or later your actions will drive them to ask, "Why?" And what greater opportunity is there to share the love of God?

God's Everlasting Love

This is God's own strategy with you and me. You see, while I was a sinner, lost in my sin, taking advantage of God, He continued to love me. While I was going my own way, not listening to Him, turning my back on Him and wanting only to do what I wanted to do, He kept on loving me. While I was rebellious and stiff-necked and I just wanted pleasure out of my life, God kept on blessing me.

He didn't worry about whether I was taking advantage of Him. He kept on loving me until one day I fell on my knees and I bowed my head and heart and I said, "God, why? Why would you love me like that; why would you bless me like that?" If God has done that for us, if He laid down His life for us when we couldn't give two hoots about Him, why can't we love some of our neighbors? Why can't we love our co-workers? Why can't we put ourselves in a position where we can make known the mystery of the gospel in an effective way?

If we're going to walk in victory, we need to understand the power that we have in Christ. We need to understand the opposition we face. We need to understand the context of the "evil day" in which we live, and we also need to have goals. The goal is to stand firm when the pressure is on us, to stand against the devil, making known the mystery of the gospel.

Prayer Is Key for Victory

Then Paul adds the critical ingredient for victory in Ephesians 6:18, *"Praying always, with all prayer and supplication in the spirit."* You see; this strategy requires prayer. You can't just walk out the door and fight the battle without prayer. The utilization of the armour of God cannot happen outside of prayer so you've got to be a praying person. You don't go into battle without good logistics and communications. You don't go to war if you're not in touch with headquarters. God is saying, "Look, you can step out into the spiritual war that's being waged, but you had better do it while maintaining good communication with me."

That's why Paul says that you've got to "pray always", to pray without ceasing. You've got to get up in the morning and establish that connection with God. Talk to Him! We need to get ourselves into a position where we don't even want to walk out the front door without having a long talk with God. Where we don't want to make any decisions in our lives without talking to God. Where we want to consult Him on every little detail.

If we're going to live that victorious life, we must have all these things: an understanding of the value of Christ in our lives, an awareness of the opposition, the knowledge that this is the evil day, a desire to have bold, "Paul-like" goals for sharing the mysteries of Christ, and to be utterly dependent on ceaseless prayer.

2
God Goes Before Us

A mother asked her little son, "Have you ever heard God speak to you while you were lying down at night in bed?" The little boy said, "Oh yeah! I hear voices all the time when I'm in bed. Mostly the voice says, "Son, go to bed!"

Sometimes we need to be a bit more like that little boy and recognize that God does speak to us, but God doesn't always speak the same way. He speaks to us in a variety of ways. Sometimes He uses other people—our mother or father, our spouse, a best friend, or even a stranger. Sometimes through our circumstances He is speaking to us. Many times we overlook the fact that God is going before us, leading us, and guiding us in a myriad of ways in our lives.

We need to walk out the door in the morning sensitive to the fact that God is there, going before us, leading us. That's what He tried to convince the Israelites when they left Egypt and entered the wilderness. He promised that He was going to go before them. They huddled in His presence at the foot of Mount Sinai, and God gave them the Ten Commandments and the laws. Then God challenged them with the fact that they had a long journey in front of them with a wilderness to cross, battles to fight and Canaanites to deal with. You might say that, like us, God let them know they had issues to deal with.

But God wanted to encourage them, as He wants to encourage us; no matter what it is that you have to face in life, He will go before you. He's into tomorrow before you get there and He'll go before you and deal with those problems even before you have to deal with them. He's working out situations that you don't even know about yet and He's working them out for your good.

God Is Sovereign and Will Keep You in the Way

In Exodus 23, an Angel of the Lord says that the Lord will go before you and keep you in the way. What does He mean that He will keep you in the way?

First of all, God is encouraging us with His sovereignty and the fact that ultimately, He is in control. The doctrine of the Perseverance of the Saints, which came out of the Reformation, is one of the important doctrines in the Bible that needs to be better understood. I would encourage us to consider this teaching in the Church. Ultimately what it comes down to is this: God is a sovereign God and everything happens by His permission. He either causes it or allows it to happen. Nothing goes down without His prior approval.

Now you may ask, "How can you make a statement like that? What about all the sin and disease and calamity in the world? What about the millions killed by Stalin? What about the thousands wiped out by volcanoes, tornadoes, hurricanes and other natural disasters? Thousands were killed when terrorists slammed two commercial passenger flights into the World Trade Center and one into the Pentagon. Did God cause that to happen?" Absolutely not! But did He allow that to happen? Absolutely yes, because nothing happens—not even sin—without God's prior permission.

I'm not saying God initiates or approves of sin, because He doesn't. He hates sin. I'm also not saying God is going to tolerate sin in your life, because He won't. What I am saying is that God has and always had a plan for sin. Even before the foundations of the world God knew what was going to happen in the Garden of Eden, but He went ahead and made the world anyhow. That needs to challenge our thinking. As we consider the fall of Adam and Eve, and thus the fall of mankind, we have to recognize that this did not startle God or catch Him off guard. The serpent in the Garden did not come out of left field at God because God is above time and space. He is at the beginning and the end and knows all that happens in the universe at the same time, all the time.

The fact is, because of His foreknowledge of the fall of man, He could write in His Word that Jesus Christ was slain before the foundations of the world. Before the foundations of the world were created, before there was a Garden of Eden, He had already figured out how He was going to save you and me. He had already laid the ground work for Jesus Christ to come and be our Saviour.

We can't minimize the sovereignty of God. We're talking about a God who is in absolute control. We're talking about a God who is in charge of heaven and earth. We're talking about a God who has His hand on everything, even in the most difficult times in life. Even those times when you can't imagine what God could possibly be working out, God is going before us. God is in that situation, and He's working it out for our good. We simply need to believe that by faith and because He says it is so. As it says in Romans 8:28, *"And we know that all things work together for good to those who love God, to those who are the called according to His purpose."*

God Has a Place Prepared for Us

He's going to go before you—but the promise here is that He's going to keep you in the way. Now, this presents some special problems. In this idea of the perseverance of the saints, one of the things expressed is that once we come to Christ and received Him as our personal Lord and Saviour, God is going to keep us and preserve us until that day when we will be in His presence in glory. That's a wonderful promise.

God doesn't have a haphazard relationship with us. He loves us, He cherishes us, and He promises that He's going to keep us. God promised the nation of Israel at Mount Sinai that He was going to keep them in the way and take them to the Promised Land, and in the same way God's agenda is to bring you into that place that He's prepared for you.

Psalm 36 paints some word pictures for us. One of the pictures I see in that passage is that of a little child sitting by the water sipping from a cup in his hands. It's a beautiful picture by the Psalmist of one sitting by the rivers of God's pleasure, sipping from all that God is.

But this is not the complete picture. The reality is that God's agenda is not to bring you to the water and give you a cup. It's not even for you to just take little sips of His goodness. God wants you to jump in! God wants you swimming in His goodness, totally immersed in Him.

There's another picture that hits a little closer to home. The Psalmist also says that we are to be totally satisfied in the house of God, totally satisfied by all the abundance and goodness of Him. You see; that's what God wants for you. God wants you totally immersed in His presence, in His house and in His goodness. What's more, He wants to personally take you there.

We Must Surrender to God

If God offers so much, why is it that we all know people who went forward, said the salvation prayer, and started living the Christian life, but a few weeks later it's as if nothing has changed and you're calling them up and asking, "What happened?" We all know people who made professions of faith and it seemed like they were walking right. In fact, we would have put our last dollar on the table and said, "This is a child of God," only to find they have fallen by the wayside.

How do you reconcile the fact that people fall away and what the Word of God has promised when the Lord says He's going to keep us in the way? If it's a matter of reconciling your perception of reality with what the Word of God is saying, you had better stand on the Word of God. Isaiah 55:8 says, *"'For My thoughts are not your thoughts, nor are your ways My ways,' says the LORD."* Let's not run away and water down the promises of God because we've got some difficult issues to reconcile in our minds.

None of us know who has really made a genuine step of faith to God. No one knows who has really dealt with God in their hearts. The Lord told Samuel in I Samuel 16:7: *"Man looks at the outward appearance, but the Lord looks at the heart."* Just because you walk into church, just because you've got all the Christian lingo down, and just because you've been teaching Sunday School for ten years doesn't mean that you have bowed your heart before God.

Here's a way you can tell if you have really surrendered your heart to God. All of us face forks in the road. I call them tests. A test is a fork in the road where God tells us to go one way but we think that blessings are waiting on another road. We think the better job, the better house, and the better situation is one way while God is telling us to go the other way.

When a Christian has surrendered his heart to God, he is saying, "God, no matter what way I think is best, if your way is different I'm going to obey you and follow you. I'm going to always do what you tell me to do."

Many times sitting in my office, I have dealt with people who are at that fork in the road. I often ask them, "Do you love Jesus?" And they will say, "Yes I do." But when we talk about the fork in the road, they can't seem to make the statement, "I want to do what God wants me to do." They almost always say, "Yes, I know its right and that's what God wants me to do, but…!" And there is always some excuse.

I don't care how long you've been in church. I don't care how many zeros you put on your offering check. It doesn't matter what else you say, if you're not at the place (and only you know) where you're willing to put God first and surrender your life to Him, then this promise is not for you. When God talks about keeping you in His way, He's talking about people who have given their lives to God, people who have surrendered their heart to Him. That's between you and God. I can't tell you that God is going to keep you in the way because I don't really know if you are surrendered to Him. I accept your profession at face value but I can't see your heart and I don't know what's going on in your head.

So it comes down to the kind of relationship you have with God. Once someone has come to the place where they've really submitted their life to Christ, God promises that He will keep them in the way. There are some good verses of Scripture to encourage us. Psalm 121:3, puts it this way, *"He will not allow your foot to be moved; He who keeps you will not slumber."* It goes on to say in verse 5, *"The Lord is your keeper."*

You see; I'm not worried about my foot being moved. I'm not worried about slipping out of the way and I'm not, as some of the gospel songs say, "Holdin' onto God." I know that God is holding onto me. I thank God that it's not my grip on God that's going to maintain my relationship with Him, He's holding onto me and He will not allow my feet to be moved. For those of us who know that we love God and have surrendered our lives to Him, this should be an encouraging word.

Fear The Lord

There are two conditions in Exodus 23, given to you to experience the leading of the Lord. Christians need to understand what the Bible means when it says, *"fear the Lord."* We need to understand that there's value in fearing God, in having reverential respect and awe for who God is. How important it is to the Christian life? Proverbs 9:10a says, *"The fear of the Lord is the beginning of wisdom."*

An interesting verse in Exodus 20:20 says, "Fear not," but in Proverbs 1:7 it says, *"Fear."* We're not to fear that God is out to get us, to destroy us. But by the same token, we are to fear God because He has come to prove us, to try us, and to test us. God is interested in making us and moulding us. That's a process that we as Christians need to respect. We need to have confidence in the love of God, but also reverence in His power and His desire to conform us into the image of His Son.

Years ago I did a Bible study with the Philadelphia Eagles, and I had the privilege of meeting a lot of fine professional athletes. One of the good Christian brothers I spent some time with was Reggie White. If you have ever been with Reggie in person, you are instantly aware that he is a huge man. Reggie White is one of those guys that when you stand in front of him you are in awe at the physical specimen that's before you. But his wife Sara is a very tiny woman. I mean short, tiny, petite; talk about the weaker vessel! To watch those two interact together, this tiny woman with this huge man, just boggles your mind.

Well, I stopped to think about that with regard to fearing God. I'm sure that Sara has a certain healthy respect for the physical power that's in Reggie. When you watch on Sundays as he plows down quarterbacks and mows down the opposition— it's enough to create a little bit of awe and respect in the power of the man. At the same time, here's this frail little woman who comes right up and nestles up under Reggie's arm. As his wife, she has no fear at all to approach him and go where quarterbacks won't dare go.

Now, why is that? She has a healthy fear of Reggie—in fact, she respects his power, but she also has just as healthy a respect for the love he has for her and the care and protection that his power enables her to experience. And that's the way we need to look at God. We need to understand the power that's there, the muscle, the sovereignty that's represented by His person. At the same time, we can approach Him with a respect for the love, the mercy, and the grace that's been extended to each one of us. We need not fear God and yet we need to fear God. We can have that same kind of respect and a healthy fear of the Lord as He goes before us and guides us along this Christian path.

We Need Humility

There is one other condition to the Lord keeping us in the way and guiding us. When the Lord goes before you He will lead you if you allow Him to lead you.

The opposite of allowing God to lead you is when we provoke God. We do this when we lack the humility necessary to simply follow His directions. We need to have humility in His presence. John Bunyan wrote, in *The Pilgrim's Progress*, "He that is humble ever will have God as his guide."

This reminds me of my children when they were younger. If I was walking along the sidewalk with my young children and I reached the corner, what did they instinctively do? They reached out and took my hand. They instinctively recognized that they were approaching a situation that was a little bit beyond them and they trusted me to carry them through that difficult circumstance.

I don't know exactly what age they were, but at some point I got to the corner and nobody grabbed my hand. In fact, my kids were running off in front of me. At some point they figured out they could handle the intersection on their own. I think that's what happens to us as Christians. We reach the place where we lose humility before God and we begin to rely on our own intellect and our own understanding.

We come to situations in life, intersections along the road of life, and we figure that we can handle it on our own. We don't have to pray about decisions as we used to and we don't come to God with minor problems anymore. That's when we begin to provoke God. Maybe God is leading us in another direction or telling us to wait because the light is yellow, yet we reject His leadership and run on ahead of Him. We need a little bit of humility to cause us to continue to hold out our hands and reach out for God's leadership in our lives.

Peggy Tehan of Dayton, Ohio was driving her small children to a skating party. After several wrong turns and receiving bad directions, she pulled the car over and told the kids, "You know what, let's pray and ask God to help us find this rink." After they prayed they found out they were just a couple of blocks and a turn away from the rink. The next time they were going to the same rink, they went out to the driveway, jumped in the car and her little 3-year old said, "Well Mom, why don't we stop and pray now and save some time!" Out of the mouth of babes come pearls of wisdom. This little child understood the principle of humbly allowing God to lead you.

God goes before us to lead us and to guide us, but we need to be like children. Luke 18:16-17 says, *"But Jesus called the children to Him and said, "Let the little children come to me, and do not hinder them, for the kingdom of God belongs to such as these. I tell you the truth, anyone who will not receive the kingdom of God like a little child will never enter it."* We need a child-like faith and humility that says to our heavenly Father, "Daddy, lead me and guide me today."

Too often we grab the circumstances and trials of life and take them into our own hands. Too often we run by sight and not by faith. We navigate by and lean on our own understanding. What we need is to get to the place where we can turn everything over to Him and keep our hand out for Him to lead us and to guide us. If we will put God up front in our lives He promises that He'll go before us and lead us. As Proverbs 3:5-6 says, *"Trust in the LORD with all your heart and lean not on your own understanding; in all your ways acknowledge him, and he will make your paths straight."*

God Forgives

There are some essential benefits that come once we are ready to let God lead us. When the Lord goes before you and is truly Lord of your life, He pardons your sins, and all of us are in need of forgiveness.

You know how little children can get dirty. Well, when you get dirty you have three options. One option is to hide the dirt — I've been there. You try and hide it so nobody can see. Another option is to deny the dirt. You'll hear little kids saying, "What cookies?" Meanwhile, the crumbs are all over their mouths. The third option is to confess the dirt and get it dealt with.

All of us need forgiveness and all of us face those three options. We can try to hide the sin, deny it, or confess it. God is willing to offer us all the forgiveness that we need, but the only option that works with God is to go to Him and confess our sin.

In 1993, British police accused two 10-year old boys of killing a 2-year old little boy named James Bugler. The boys denied it to the police until the parents of one of the boys came in and talked to their 10-year old son. They told him, "Son, we'll love you no matter what you did. Just be honest and tell them you did it. We'll love you anyhow." With all the mounting evidence against them and the strength given to them by the unconditional love of these parents, the boys got the courage to confess to the police the crime that they committed.

The great miracle of our salvation is that God is willing to forgive us even though He already knows every bad thing we've committed. There are some things in your life you might think you have all wrapped up nice and tight, that nobody else knows about. There are some secrets you might think you're walking around with that nobody else knows. But God knows it all and there is no way you can outrun your need for God's forgiveness. God is willing to forgive you no matter what you've done, no matter what your situation is. Isaiah 55:7 says, *"Let the wicked forsake his way and the evil man his thoughts. Let him turn to the* LORD, *and He will have mercy on him, and to our God, for He will freely pardon."* And I John 1:9, *"If we confess our sins, He is faithful and just and will forgive us our sins and purify us from all unrighteousness."* That's something that all of us can grab onto.

God Fights Our Battles

Notice also that when the Lord goes before you He will also fight your battles. It doesn't say anywhere in God's Word that He will eliminate your battles. The Christian life is not a magic carpet ride or a life of ease. There are some battles to fight. God told the Israelites they were going to have to deal with Canaanites, Perizzites, and Hivites. Taking possession of the Promised Land would not come without a fight, and in life there will be battles. But God is saying He will go before you and fight the battles for you.

We have the victory in Jesus, but we also have all these battles and situations to deal with in life. We need, as Christians, to get to the place where we can look beyond our current circumstances and have faith and trust that the ultimate battle will be won in Christ Jesus.

I'm a sports fanatic, and I once read a story about a game between the Michigan State football team and Wisconsin. Michigan State came into the Wisconsin stadium and was kicking them up and down the field. The Wisconsin team was really getting beat badly but the fans were cheering louder and louder as the game went on. The announcer couldn't understand what was going on until he realized that a lot of the fans had radios with headphones and they were listening to the Milwaukee Brewers winning game three of the World Series. All the fans with headphones were listening to a winning game and cheering every time something good happened to the Brewers.

There's a valuable lesson for us here. We, like those fans, shouldn't get down in the dumps by the situation that's right in front of us. The Wisconsin fans were able to look past the current situation and see what was happening somewhere far away, something outside of their eyesight. And it gave them a chance to cheer.

Put on your spiritual headphones and listen to His winning voice. It doesn't matter what we're facing on a day-to-day basis.

We should be tuned into a whole different station and a whole different battle. It's a battle that God is winning and ultimately it's going to be shown in every one of our circumstances.

You might be in the middle of the battle today. Satan might be kicking you up and down the street and you might be getting your head knocked in by the circumstances you are going through. But we need to be tuned into a more important ball game, because there's a spiritual battle taking place and it's a battle that we, as Christians, are winning. The ultimate victory is ours regardless of the current circumstances. God wants to encourage you not to be bogged down by obsessing these battles right around you and to trust Him that the final victory is yours.

Jesus Is All We Need

In 1991, when the Eagles actually had a good team, they called Randall Cunningham "the ultimate weapon." They went into every game feeling confident because they had "the ultimate weapon" on their side. In the spiritual battle that's raging in this world, we've got more than "the ultimate weapon." We've got the perfect sacrifice! Jesus Christ is the King of Kings and He's garbed in righteousness. He is the Master of the stormy sea. Jesus is the one who triumphed over death and the grave. We have the victory.

When the Apostle Paul was writing to the church in Rome, he said, *"If God is for us, who can be against us?"* (Rom. 8:31) You should be clicking your heels! Even though there's a high stack of bills on your desk, you can rejoice through it all. Even though your boss is getting down on you and grinding his heel on the top of your head, you can smile and have joy because we can pick up the Word of God and get the play-by-play on a far more important level of the battle where we are experiencing the victory.

God Provides Your Needs

Another benefit you have when the Lord goes before you is that He will meet all of your physical needs. He promised the Israelites that He would bless their bread, bless their water, and remove their sickness. God is involved with His people in the physical realm. He promised Israel that He would meet their physical needs, give them a home and that their nation would be a blessing. The question is, how do these promises relate to us and what does God promise to us in a physical sense?

One thing that clears this whole dilemma up is some clear teaching in the New Testament. In Matthew chapter 6, Jesus tells us that His heavenly Father, the sovereign God, is in charge of heaven and earth. We don't need to worry about what we have to eat, the clothes on our back, the physical things that we need in life because God is taking care of that. If His eye is on the needs of the sparrow, certainly His eye is going to be on you and me.

Jesus didn't shed His blood for the grass on the field or the ecosystem, but He did die for you and for me because of His unfathomable love for us. His promise to us is that He will meet all of our needs and will take care of us regardless of where we find ourselves.

Maybe you're in between jobs, facing medical crises, the loss of your business, or just going through the ongoing trials of life. No matter what the strains in life, we need to come to it understanding that God goes before us, leading and guiding us. He's in all the ups and the downs. He's in all the turns and the curves. Life might not play out the way we think it should, but God is in the midst of it all. He says that through it all, He's going to see to it that all of our needs are met.

> "Now the disciples had forgotten to take bread, and they did not have more than one loaf with them in the boat. Then He charged them, saying, 'Take heed, beware of the leaven of the Pharisees and the leaven of Herod.' And they reasoned among themselves, saying, 'It is because we have no bread.' But Jesus, being aware of it, said to them, 'Why do you reason because you have no bread? Do you not yet perceive nor understand? Is your heart still hardened? Having eyes, do you not see? And having ears, do you not hear? And do you not remember? When I broke the five loaves for the five thousand, how many baskets full of fragments did you take up?' They said to Him, 'Twelve.' 'Also, when I broke the seven for the four

thousand, how many large baskets full of fragments did you take up?' And they said, 'Seven.' So He said to them, 'How is it you do not understand?'" (Mark 8:14-21).

Jesus is not concerned about how much money you have in the bank. Your security is not about how many pieces of bread you have in your lunch pail, whether your union status is OK or what the quality of your relationship is with your employer. It's not in how much (or how little) you have in your bank account or how big your pension fund is. Jesus is saying to you and to me, "Don't you get it? If I can miraculously provide for five thousand people using only five loaves of bread, if you have Me, you have all you need!" The disciples complained about having one loaf of bread in the boat, but they had Jesus in the boat. When you have Jesus in your life, all of the security you will ever need is in your relationship with Him. Your security is Jesus.

3
Keep Your Hands Up

Ask any boxer and he'll tell you one of the most important things to do when you go into a fight is to keep your hands up. I remember in the schoolyards of elementary and junior high school when we used to do what we called "slap boxing." Most of the action was to your head and you had to keep your hands up or your opponent would slap you silly. In a fight, if you lower your hands you've lost the battle.

The Enemy is Coming

I believe that is what God is telling us in Exodus 17, 8–16. In these verses you can read the wonderful account of the battle between the Amalekites and the Israelites at Rephidim. As God's people traveled through the wilderness and into the Promised Land, one of the enemies that kept cropping up was the Amalekites. They represent for us all of the enemies we face, the enemies of God and the world system. Time and again the people of Israel found themselves in a fight against the heathen, godless nations of the world.

First of all, Moses sent Joshua and his chosen men into the battle. God doesn't take us out of the difficulties of life. On the contrary, He orders us into battle but promises to provide the power to win. As Joshua and his men fought the enemy, Moses went up on top of a hill and held up the rod of God. Verse 11 says, *"And so it was, when Moses held up his hand, that Israel prevailed; and when he let down his hand, Amalek prevailed."*

As the day and the battle wore on, Moses' legs and arms

grew tired. He had to sit down and God provided Aaron and Hur to stand on each side and hold up his hands and the rod of God. In our lives, the Lord will provide the people and the provisions we need when we grow weary from the battle. The lesson to remember is that all of us are in a spiritual battle and if we drop our hands, if we don't step out in faith and hold up the rod of God, we're going to get hit and hit hard.

The Amalekites are not around any more, the Lord took care of them as He promised to do, but we still have an enemy. The words of Martin Luther in one of the greatest hymns ever written, "A Mighty Fortress is our God," point out that we are in a fight and we have a foe with no equal here on earth. The Devil is in a continuous spiritual battle to destroy the Church. Just as Moses didn't give up, didn't surrender, so the Church must put on the whole armour of God, with our hands up at all times, ready to fight.

We Need To Fight

The apostle Paul encourages us in I Timothy 1:18 to *"Fight the good fight,"* or "Wage the good warfare." We need to stop being passive Christians and to be willing to stand up for Christ and His truth even when people think you've lost a screw. People will be offended when you publicly praise the Lord for all that you have and all that He is in your life. But we must stand up and fight for the One who gave His life to save us.

The Bible tells us how to fight against the devil and against the world system. In Ephesians 6:11, when Paul tells us to, *"Put on the whole armour of God,"* he's not talking about buying physical guns and armour. What he is talking about is utilizing the spiritual arsenal of faith. His list of weapons includes truth, righteousness, peace, faith, salvation, the Word, and prayer. These are the weapons we need to fight in our every day pursuits.

The fight is not about another dollar from the federal government. It is not over wider streets and longer highways. The fight is against the devil and the world system. In a democracy, one method Christians can use to make their voices heard and fight for God's moral standard is in the voting booth. We need to get registered and vote. And when we vote, we can no longer leave our Christianity in church and walk into the voting booth and forget what the fight is all about.

We should be out there, fighting the good fight within our communities. Every time they hold a city council meeting in your town, you should be there with fellow Christians, making your voices heard. We should be out in force creating pro-life rallies that share the biblical view against abortion. Every time a school board meeting is held the Christians need to stand up and bring forth policies that honour God's standards of right and wrong for our children. We should be fighting the fight whether it is in public or at the dinner table with our families.

Some Christians like to take sides and preach politics. I'm not going to do that and I won't tell you what party to align yourself with, whether Republican, Democrat, Reformed, Libertarian or whatever other tag you want to put on yourself. Regardless of all those labels, the one thing every Christian should be able to rally around is God's Word and His moral standard. Let's fight the fight, first and foremost, for God's Kingdom, and let's not be passive about it.

We're In the Wrong Fight

Many of us are just too busy with other battles to battle for the Kingdom. We're fighting the fight for a brand new car, new threads or a bigger house. We may be fighting the overtime fight or just struggling to keep our heads above water. But we're fighting for everything but God's Kingdom and His glory. We need to devote time and energy fighting the good fight and running the race that glorifies God. We have a debt to God. Our time on earth is short. That Apostle Paul said that our lives are not our own, we were bought with a price. That price was the very life of Christ, so that when our time here is finished we will spend eternity in heaven.

When Joshua was sent to battle against the Amalekites, notice how he was obedient to Moses. We don't find any excuses in Joshua. We don't read, "I have to go home and think about it." He didn't have to rearrange his priorities. Moses told Joshua to *"Choose us some men and go out, fight with Amalek. Tomorrow I will stand on the top of the hill with the rod of God in my hand"* And that's what Joshua did. As it says in the next verse, *"So Joshua did as Moses said to him, and fought Amalek."* Joshua obeyed Moses immediately and the result was a battle won. It's no different for us. If we want to see God's power at work in our lives, we have to be obedient.

I know that for some of you, reading this book is not going to make much of a difference. Your priorities are still going to be the same and you're not going to change a thing. You will continue to make decisions about your priorities and the use of your time that will take you out of the battle. But I believe there are some who will see the vision God has given to His people. You will get actively involved in the spiritual battle and will make the necessary changes in your life to make a contribution to the Kingdom of God. It is for you that this book is written.

Be Willing to Take a Stand

There should be more men in this world like Bill Devlin, President of the Urban Family Council. Here is a brilliant man who has stepped out and taken on the world system, speaking out publicly against problems like abortion, child molestation, gambling and the breakdown of the family and working to educate and to build interracial and cross-cultural partnerships in Philadelphia.

As a result, Devlin has been harassed on calls to his home and he has gotten death threats. The gay rights community has put up posters with Bill's picture all around the city. Bill Devlin has put himself on the line. Why? He's bold and obedient enough to believe that he should be standing for God's standard.

There needs to be more of that. God is rising up a remnant that is willing to fight for what they believe. This is a handful of the faithful who aren't going to just flow down the river wherever the stream takes them. The faithful camp is the camp I'm in, what about you? Are you willing to stand up and fight for God's standard?

Have the Right Perspective for Battle

Joshua went out to the battle as Moses had instructed him to do and Moses, Aaron and Hur went up to the top of the hill.

They needed to get a broader perspective of the battle. They needed to go to a high place where they could get a good view of all that was going on down in the valley.

A good leader doesn't get bogged down in all the details. He or she has to be able to see the battle from a broader perspective. Moses recognized that so he didn't pick up a sword. He didn't run out to the front line of the battle. Our lives are no different. You can't get all bogged down in every swing of the devil and every detail of the fight. When you spend time with God and seek His counsel He takes you up to a high place where He can give you the big picture.

I had lunch recently with a local pastor who has been at his church for about three and a half years. He came into a church that had about 25 or 30 people in it and they expected him to do everything. He has to preach Sunday morning, Sunday night, and at the Wednesday night Bible study. They can't afford a secretary so he prepares the bulletin and during the week he's out doing all the visitations. He's completely bogged down in all the details. In his frustration he told me over lunch, "I'm wearing myself out! I'm working 60 hours a week and after three and half years there's still only about 30 people in the church."

I asked him, "What would happen if one week you didn't prepare a bulletin and instead you took that time and went out on street corners or to the shopping mall and handed out some invitations to people? What would happen if there was no bulletin but there were visitors who came to the church?" He said, "Well, I can tell you what would happen. There would be church members up in arms, asking, "Where's the bulletin? What are we paying this guy for?" So many pastors become ineffective because they are caught up in doing the non-essential details that are expected of them instead of focusing on the essentials of the Kingdom.

Do God's Work

We are all leaders in some sphere and we all have people who are watching us and want to make demands on our time. If the expectations of others bog you down you will never be successful. We need to put those aside and do what God has called us to do. Some of Joshua's soldiers, walking down to the battle with swords in hand, were probably asking, "Where's Moses going? We're putting our lives on the line and he's walking up the hill." But in order to be a good leader, you can't be led by people's expectations. People will run you ragged and when you drop they'll walk away. It's only God who will never leave you, and it's only God who will sustain you. When it comes to deciding how to live your life, "go up on the hill" and seek first to please the Lord.

Prayer Is the Key

When Moses raised his hands and the rod of God above the Israelites battle with the Amalekites, it wasn't just some abstract gesture in obedience to God. In the Old Testament, when Abraham and others did a swearing, they stretched out their hands and put it on somebody's thigh to signify an oath. It was a ritual making a promise to God. If you translated Moses' "swearing," literally in the Hebrew, it says his "hand was upon the throne of the Lord."

Moses was stretching his hands up to the throne of God in prayer. He was appealing to God. Moses could see that the Amalekites were much stronger than his army and that Joshua and his men, a little rag-tag army that had not been properly equipped since they left Egypt, would surely be wiped out. Yet, Moses also knew that God was able, God was powerful. So he stretched out his hands to the throne of God. It was a prayer, appealing to God to rescue them against overwhelming odds and give them the victory.

Look at the results. Perspective is good, but prayer brings the victory. It's one thing to step aside from the battle, see all the problems and strategize, but without prayer all of that is useless. A good leader has to be honest in recognizing when the battle is way over his head and that he needs God to fight the fight for him. So he stretches out his hands as Moses did and appeals to God.

Notice that every time Moses got tired of praying, tired of holding up his hands to the throne of God, the Amalekites gained the upper hand in the battle. And every time his hands went up and he started praying again, the Israelites were winning. That's why you need to keep your hands up when you're in the fight. You need to keep on praying. It is essential for us to be people of prayer. We must be people that see that prayer brings the victory. So keep your hands up when you're in the battle.

Aaron and Hur understood how important prayer was and when Moses' arms got tired, what did they do? They grabbed his arms and held them up for him. Aaron and Hur understood that they had to keep this man praying or the battle would be lost. Moses surrounded himself with people who understood the value of prayer. Look around you. Do those closest to you value prayer and the need to have God's power for the victory? Do they encourage you to pray in every situation? How different our lives would be if we were men and women of prayer and surrounded ourselves with prayer warriors!

We're not in a schoolyard slap-boxing match where you're not allowed to make a fist and the consequences of losing the fight are small. Satan is out to tear you down and to destroy you. As we're learning from this biblical story, we're involved in a spiritual battle and we better keep our hands up in prayer because it is as you continue in prayer that you prevail. When you stop praying, you're going to get knocked out of the ring, and when the arena is your life, the stakes don't get any higher. You must prevail in prayer.

Remember Who is on the Throne

Moses stretched out his hands to the throne of the Lord. The throne is where our King sits, it signifies His rule, and it reminds us that He's in charge.

Effective prayer recognizes that God is in charge of our lives. Effective prayer says, just as Christ Himself said, *"Not as I will, but as You will"* (Matt. 26:39)

It's not about me, it's about Him. What did Jesus say in John 14:13? *"And whatever you ask in My name, that I will do, that the Father may be glorified in the Son."* It's about glorifying the Lord. So many times we come to prayer like God is some kind of vending machine. Every time we throw in a prayer we expect our wish to pop out. But prayer is not about you! When we stretch out our hands in prayer we need to recognize that we are reaching out to the very throne of God, recognizing that He is King of Kings and Lord of Lords, the Sovereign God. It's all about Him. When we pray, *"Not my will but thy will be done,"* we're not watering down the faith, we are praying as we only have the right to pray. It's not about our will. He is the Lord.

When I say I have faith in God, it means that God has said something that I have confidence in. It implies that God has spoken. If I decide to jump out the window and I have faith that I'm not going to break my leg, since I know God didn't tell me He was going to spare me from breaking my leg, what am I having faith in? I'm not having faith in God, I'm having faith in my own imagination, in what I have concocted in the flesh.

Real faith has to be based on what God has said. When I have faith in God, I am standing on His promises and having confidence in what He has said. When God says it, I believe it, and that settles it. That's faith. Faith is not wishful thinking. Faith believes God and His Word and what He's told us.

When I stretch my hands out to the throne of God, recognizing that He's in charge, I'm opening up the lines of faith so God can speak to me. Whatever He tells me to do, that's what I'll do. Whatever He tells me is His plan, that's what I'll roll with. That's faith. Faith is when we have confidence in God, even when we don't see it, even when it's all we can do just to hope for it. Why? Because we have confidence in what God has said. As it says Hebrews 11:1, *"Now faith is the substance of things hoped for, the evidence of things not seen."*

The Lord Is Our Banner

This concept of faith and reaching out to the throne of God is reinforced by the name of the altar that Moses built. Exodus 17, verse 15 says, *"And Moses built an altar and called its name, Jehovah Nissi, the Lord is my banner."* "Nissi" simply means, "my banner." If you were to put it in today's culture, *Nissi* is like a flag that everybody rallies under and shows allegiance to.

Now get the picture. Here is Moses, appealing to the sovereign God on His throne, giving God the right to do whatever He wants to do. It's his version of, *"Not my will, but Thine be done."* Then Moses builds an altar and he says the name of this altar is, "I give my allegiance to the flag of the one true God." He is saying, "I owe all to Him—all my allegiance, all my devotion, all my love, and all my worship. I'm even willing to give up my life for Him." That's the statement being made by "Jehovah Nissi", the flag of God.

I'm as much a patriot as anybody else. I stood in grade school with all the other kids, put my hand over my heart and said, "I pledge allegiance to the flag of the United States of America, and to the Republic for which it stands ... " If you grew up in America you can probably say it with your eyes closed and backwards, you've said it so many times.

But the flag I really want to rally around more than any other is the one that I want to give my primary allegiance to. It's "Jehovah Nissi". I want to rally around that flag and I would give my life to that flag. As Christians, we ought to make our pledge of allegiance, "I pledge allegiance to the flag of Jehovah Nissi, the Lord is my banner, and to His Church for which He died, one Church, indivisible, with the Gospel of Salvation for all." I believe that's what our heart pledge should be. We need to rally and to pledge our allegiance to Him and to His Church.

Pledge to Live for Christ

Are you willing to give your all and allegiance to Him? Are you willing to fight in the battle under His banner? Will you lay down your life for Him as Jesus laid down His life for you? God is making an appeal to each one of us to put away all of our own ambitions and desires and pledge allegiance to God first and foremost. He's calling us to say to the world, "The Lord, He is Lord! He is my banner and I will fight under His flag!"

Moses message, "Keep your hands up", means you must step out in faith and enter the battle, keeping your hands up in prayer, recognizing that it's the throne of God and His rule that will prevail. Keeping your hands up is not about waving your hands in the air because the music is good or the choir is singing. This is about raising our hands to Him in prayer and saying, "Lord, take me. I surrender. You're in charge. You call the shots. All to Jesus. I give Him everything. I give Him all my money. I give Him all my time. And if You give me back a little to use for myself, that's all well and good. But Lord, You take my life, my family situation, my kids, my money, my job, my week, and You do with them whatever You want."

"Keep your hands up" also means praying without ceasing. It means spending time with Him when you're tired, when you're sick, and when you're sick and tired! It's not letting your hands drop because as your hands fall you begin to lose the battle. If you can keep your hands stretched out to God you will see the Lord prevail. Perhaps we will be prompted to stretch out our hands to the throne of God when we truly realize that if there is going to be victory in the battle then the sovereign God has to provide it.

I wonder, how many of us are really ready to submit to God like that and do whatever He says? How many of us are willing to break off ungodly relationships? How many will reconcile with that brother or sister who has offended us, or spend time in ministry we know we're supposed to be doing and give back to God the gifts He's given to us to edify His Church? We need to be willing to fight, to rally under that flag, "Jehovah Nissi, the Lord is my banner," and give up our all to Him.

4
God Leads In Every Situation

Once there was a man who was riding his motorcycle along a South Georgia highway on a summer night. As he was driving, the highway lights on top of the poles mesmerized him. If you ever drive at night, you know that the stripes in the middle of the road and the lights can have a hypnotic effect. The motorcyclist got so caught up with these lights that he focused on just watching the lights go by. He was able to steer because the lights were running parallel to the road. All of a sudden the road took a sharp left turn and the poles kept going straight. As you can imagine, he wound up in the hospital with multiple injuries asking the question "Why didn't the poles turn with the road?"

Sometimes we are like that man. We become so mesmerized by the things we guide our lives by, only to find that life sometimes takes a quick left turn. There is a chapter in the Bible, Exodus 13, which illustrates for us that God is in the business of leading us in every situation. He is in the business of guiding us, of steering us through life. Sometimes the lights, the flash, and the things around us distract us so that when God takes a quick left turn we find ourselves running off the road.

God Knows Where To Lead

Exodus 13 tells us that there are some things God leads you around, such as circumstances that He recognizes you are not ready for. This happened when Pharaoh let the people go and God did not lead them by the way of the land of the Philistines, although that was the nearest and fastest route. *"God said, 'If they face war, they might change their minds and return to Egypt'"* (Ex. 13:17). The road to the Philistines was like the turnpike to the land of Canaan. It was called "the Kings Highway." It was the old trade route between Egypt and Mesopotamia and it went right through the land of Canaan—the land God had promised them.

It definitely would have been the easiest and fastest way for them to get to where they were going, but God knew it would also take them through the land of the Philistines who were a war-like people. There was no way that the Philistines were going to let the Israelites just march through their land. There would be conflict and war and God knew the Israelites were not ready yet for that. He understood the condition of their faith and where their minds were and He understands the same about you. He knows what you can and cannot handle.

God Knows What We Need

There are some problems and circumstances God leads you around that you never even see and what we can't see is hard for us to appreciate. It's hard to appreciate the car accident we never had, or the bad experience that could have happened on the job we didn't get. We just have to accept by faith that there are some problems and situations that God leads us around and thank Him for it.

Not only are there problems that God leads us around, but there are also some situations He leads us through. As Paul writes, *"The Lord will rescue me from every evil attack and will bring me safely to His heavenly kingdom"* (2 Tim. 4:18). You will have problems but never more than you can bear. This is a part of God's love and care for His people.

"So God led the people around by the desert road toward the Red Sea" (Ex. 13:18). God led the people away from the Philistines, but the Israelites had another problem in front of them. If you've ever watched the movie, "Prince of Egypt", there's a pretty graphic and colourful depiction of the fact that the Israelites were trapped with the Red Sea out in front of them. For them it was an insurmountable problem. How were they going to cross the sea? This was enough to cause anyone to pull their

hair out and to question God, yet God led them there. What could they do?

The first concept to understand is that God was leading them. Even though it seemed an insurmountable problem and that they were up a creek without a paddle, God was leading them and He would see them through. That is why I can appreciate Psalm 23:4, *"Yea, though I walk through the valley of the shadow of death, I will fear no evil for thou art with me and thy rod and thy staff they comfort me."* No matter what you are facing, no matter what circumstances you are going through, God can lead you through.

Stay Attached to God

When Satan tells you that you're all alone and nobody cares; when he says you've got to pull this one off by yourself, you can tell Satan that He's a liar. God is leading you through no matter what circumstances you face. When mountain climbers attempt to climb a great peak, they usually have a guide. Do you know what the experienced guide does with the person following them up the mountain? The guide takes his or her own rope, latches it onto a D-ring and straps it on to the person following them. Wherever the guide goes, the climber goes too.

We need to be like the climber when we're going through a difficult circumstance. We need to become fastened to our guide, strapped to Jesus. The more desperate the circumstances the closer we need to tie ourselves to Him. Unfortunately, when we go through problems we tend to lose our faith, and thereby we lose our close tie with God. We even lose our desire to stay close to God and many times we start running in the other direction.

Take His Hand

I read a story about a Mr. Cinke from Scotland who took his 3 or 4 year-old son walking. The winters there were very cold with icy sidewalks. As he and his son approached a patch of ice on the sidewalk, he went to grab his son's hand. But his son pulled his hand back and said, "No, no" like a proud little boy, "I can do it." Of course the boy's feet went into the air and he landed on his backside with a painful sting.

Guess what happened the next time they came to a patch of ice? The little boy's hand was up in the air waiting for his daddy to grab it. We need to walk through life with our hands in the air waiting for God to grab us, to lead us and to guide us.

We're so proud that we think we can go through life on our own. That's why we end up on our backsides and wonder why. But if we would recognize that God always wants to lead and guide us, He could carry us through the difficulties or guide us around them. We can walk through life every day with our hands in the air saying "Daddy, take my hand. Take my life, lead me and guide me." God wants to lead you in all circumstances and no matter what you face, God is right there.

Trusting Him Brings Peace

There was a jet fighter pilot who shared his testimony about trying to land his plane on an aircraft carrier on a windy, rough, stormy day in the Pacific. The boat was rocking and rolling in the ocean and after returning from a mission the pilots were having a hard time landing. This particular pilot tried about six times and couldn't land. Then he began to run out of fuel and he had to make a decision. He had just enough fuel to do one of two things. He could either climb up to an altitude high enough to hit the eject button and save his life or he could use up the fuel trying one more time to land. If he missed this time he wouldn't be able to climb back up high enough for his parachute to open and to land safely.

As he was contemplating what to do, he said a calm and an assurance came over him that God was going to be with him and that he should try to put the jet down on the aircraft carrier. He says that during the landing an absolute peace came over him and he felt as though there was another hand on that stick leading and guiding every maneuver that he was making. As the plane sat down safely on the landing deck he was able to rejoice that God had lead him through.

God's Word teaches us clearly that He leads us and guides us through every circumstance we face. I don't know what trials or circumstances you're facing as you read this. Every one of us has a different life ahead, but God will take your hand and He will lead you through, whether it's the valley of death, sickness, depression or seemingly impossible setbacks. With God we can always pass through every trial and go on to victory.

There Is a Way

1 Corinthians 10:13 says, *"No temptation falls on us but that which is common to everyone and He won't place more on us than we can bear. But with the temptation He makes the way of escape."* God knows what you can handle and He is not naïve about the temptations the devil will throw at you. God may lead you right smack into problems and allow you to face great temptations but He will also lead you right through. With every problem and every temptation you face, there is a way of escape, I call the Victory Ramp.

Things may be falling apart in your home life and in the most important relationships in your life. Your company may be downsizing and you are out of a job, or you may own your own business and you don't know how you will last another month. Your finances may be in a disastrous condition, or you may have serious health problems. Regardless of the circumstance, when times are tough God puts signs in our life that point to the Victory Ramp. It's not hidden. It stares us in the face and if we take it, God will lead us up the Victory Ramp to a positive outcome.

We Need to Stay in Line

Since God is leading us, we need to be disciplined and carefully follow him. Exodus 13:18 says, *"God led the people around by way of the wilderness of the Red Sea and the children of Israel went up in orderly ranks."* This is the way it reads in the New King James Version, but in the old King James version, instead of using "orderly ranks", it uses the word, "harness". Let me try to clarify the difference.

When we read "orderly ranks" we think of a group of people in military order, armed and ready for battle. But most biblical scholars believe the term here, whether "harnessed" or "orderly ranks" simply means that the people of Israel were disciplined and lined up for the journey. They were not some massive mob flying helter-skelter out of Egypt. They went out of Egypt and right up to the Red Sea in orderly ranks. Everybody was where he or she was supposed to be and where God had put them; that requires discipline.

For you to stay in your rank and to follow God's leading in the midst of your problems requires a certain amount of discipline. When you face hardships you can't afford to fall out of the ranks. I am the first one to raise my hand and admit it's hard, but we must be disciplined as the people of God if we're going to be lined up where we're supposed to be and to follow Him.

That means that even though sometimes it seems hard, we've got to be in church on a regular basis. A little bit of bad weather or inconvenience can't be such a challenge that it takes us out of the ranks. We need to be disciplined and maintain a consistent personal Bible study. We need to pray daily over a list of the needs that God has put on our hearts. The whole Christian life is a life of discipline. It's a life of being where God wants you to be, and doing what God wants you to do. Too many times we allow the circumstances in our lives, the problems we face, even the inconvenience of having to roll out of bed in the morning to pull us out of the ranks.

Be encouraged with the thought that God is leading and guiding you both through and around things so you will have a positive outcome. Jeremiah 29:11 says, *"'For I know the plans I have for you,' declares the Lord, 'plans to prosper you and not to harm you, plans to give you hope and a future.'* And be aware that He's always there, always leading you. *"I will never leave you or forsake you."* (Josh. 1:5) And in verse 9, *"The Lord God will be with you wherever you go."* God is all-powerful, all-knowing and ever present. He loves us, wants the best for us and will never leave us. We need to follow God with discipline and not allow anything to come in the way of His leading in our lives.

If a friend comes over and wants to get us out of step with God, we need to say a simple "No" and keep on following Jesus. If your employer flashes some money in front of you and says a little overtime on Sunday morning or the night of the prayer meeting or Bible study will solve all your problems, if it's going to take you out of rank, just say "No thanks" and trust God to provide and keep marching on following Jesus. We must stay in the ranks if we are to experience the victory. We need to be where we're supposed to be. God wants us to be harnessed, to be in rank and strapped in, like the climber who stays strapped to his guide. Don't let anything take you out of the place where God wants you to be.

No Need to Be Blind

So often we stumble around in life, wandering from day to day and taking what comes, *que sera, sera*. All the while God is trying to lead us, guide us and help us make progress. We stumble into relationships and we end up marrying whoever we meet. We stumble into occupations and business partnerships that God never intended us to be in.

We're like the little 3-year-old slipping and sliding on the ice while his father is offering his hand to him. Our lives are spent stumbling around rather than allowing God to lead us and guide us. All the while God is calling us to a disciplined life, a life taking His hand and following His lead. Since God wants to lead us but we tend to forget His guidance is available, we also need to utilize all of our reminders.

God Never Forgets

In Genesis 50:24-25, Joseph told the people that God would visit them and deliver them from Egypt. He told them that when he died they were not to bury him in Egypt, but to carry his bones on the journey so he could be buried with his fathers—Abraham, Isaac, and Jacob—in the land of Canaan.

> *"Moses took the bones of Joseph with him because Joseph had made the sons of Israel swear an oath. He had said, 'God will surely come to your aid, and then you must carry my bones up with you from this place.' So Moses took the bones of Joseph with him"* (Ex. 13:19).

Those bones were a physical sign and a daily reminder to the children of Israel. Every time they went through hardship and testing in the wilderness, they could see Joseph's bones and remember the promise. While Joseph had died in Egypt, God promised to bring them all out and that those bones would make it to Canaan.

We've been given some bones to carry today which remind us that God loves us and He wants to carry out His plans in our lives. One of those bones is the Lord's Table. God has given us a remembrance of Himself in practical, visible symbols. Those symbols shout at us every time we participate in communion. They yell, "God loves you! God cares about you so much that He was willing to sacrifice Himself and to shed His own precious blood!"

How many people do you have in your life that would give up his or her life for you? But you've got a Guide today, someone who has already willingly laid down His life for you. Jesus wants you to follow Him and carry with you the reminders of His love so that you'll never forget.

The Lord's Table is one of those reminders, but there are other 'bones' we should carry around. How about regular corporate worship and the fellowship of the saints? God has placed His people around us to remind us to follow Him. He has given us a wealth of inspired and inspirational songs to sing that tell of His great love and sacrifice and victory for us.

We have both individual and corporate Bible Study where we can relish the opportunity to open up and sink our teeth into the Word of God. Many prefer to sleep-in rather than get up early and go out on Sunday morning for church. They prefer to watch the TV than to go to the mid-week Bible study. They walk through life with so few reminders that they easily forget that God is good and that He cares about them and wants to lead them. By Thursday afternoon they are found wandering, stumbling and slipping on the ice.

If you think about the Israelites, these bones were an extra burden to them. They had enough stuff to carry out of Egypt. I'm sure some people in the crowd wondered, "What in the world are we doing lugging around Joseph's coffin? This is a lot of dead weight on an already difficult journey!" (Ex. 50:26) There are many times in the Christian life when God will ask us to do things that seem like dead weight. It makes sense to carry every reminder we can that God will lead us, guide us and loves us, but in our own fleshly wisdom we often rationalize that we can do without reminders. We think things are all right the way they are.

The issue isn't whether you can do a good job leading your own life. The issue and the question to ask is this: Who is on the throne of your life? The issue is really one of Lordship. God didn't say, "If you need My help, just give me a call." No, He said, *"I am the Lord your God… you shall have no other God's before Me"* (Ex. 20:1-2) When we run our own lives, aren't we really putting ourselves on the throne? Be obedient. Trust God and remember that He loves you and cares about you and He is on your side. You don't need to stumble through life, just hold out your hand like a child and follow Him.

Follow with Every Sense

God is leading and we can follow him with all of our senses. *"By day the Lord went ahead of them in a pillar of cloud to guide them on their way and by night in a pillar of fire to give them light, so that they could travel by day or night. Neither the pillar of cloud by day nor the pillar of fire by night left its place in front of the people"* (Ex. 13:21-22).

When you stop to think about it, the fire and the cloud must have involved almost every sense they had. Their sight was involved in following God as He led them through. They could hear the roar of the fire and their sense of touch was involved as they felt the warmth that the fire provided for them. Their smell was no doubt involved from having a fire directly above them. If one sense gave up on them they could rely on one of the others and together it must have been an awesome experience of God's leading. A blind or deaf man could follow the warmth or the sound or the smell. If someone started to walk out from under that cloud or that fire he or she would immediately feel the difference. What's more, the fire and the cloud never left its place in front of the people. And neither does God ever leave you.

We need to get up in the morning and with every sense be tuned in to the Holy Spirit and where He is leading us. Paul says, *"Walk in the Spirit, and you will not gratify the lust of the flesh"*

(Gal. 5:16) We need to be so in tune with the Holy Spirit that even if for a little while we get out from under the cover, it hits us like walking out in the freezing cold without an overcoat.

God loves you and He cares about you, but we are so prone to walking out on our own and leaving Him behind. We need to offer up our hands to Him like a helpless child. We need to ask Him to grab hold of us and tug at us, maybe a little bit harder than we feel is comfortable. I believe He is tugging at us all the time, leading us and He's guiding us all the time. Praise God, for His mercy is everlasting and He will never leave us or forsake us.

5
Follow the Cloud

One day while I was sick in bed watching a football game I saw one of the pre-game shows that featured a heavy metal group singing the song, "Crawling in the Darkness." That seems to be the cry of so many in our world today. Life is so much like crawling in the darkness, not knowing where we're going, not knowing where life is taking us or where we're headed. We can feel that there is nobody to direct us or lead us or guide us.

We find in Numbers 9:15-23 the story of the Israelites preparing to begin their journey in the wilderness. It reminds us that we don't have to crawl in the darkness. Even when we feel lost in the wilderness, we can remember that God always provides direction for His people. Our job, like theirs, is simply to follow the cloud.

God Is Present

"And on the day that the tabernacle was raised up, the cloud covered the tabernacle, the tent of the testimony, from evening until morning it was above the tabernacle like the appearance of fire" (Num. 9:15). When the cloud covered the Tent of Meeting and the glory of the Lord, the Shekina glory, filled the Tabernacle, even Moses, who regularly communicated with God and who spoke God's commands to the Israelites, was not allowed to enter the Tent of Meeting. (Ex. 40:34-35).

To the Israelites, the tabernacle represented the presence of God. His presence was with them. He wasn't a far away God, a God that was out in the universe somewhere. He was a God who came right into their midst and showed up in the tabernacle. But the Israelites had to sacrifice in order to build a place where God could meet them. We see in Exodus 35 how they turned in their gold jewelry and ornaments, their silver and bronze and onyx stones, spices and olive oil, fine linen and hides, and the work of their most skilled craftsmen and women. Constructing the tabernacle was a great sacrifice to the people. Once the sacrifice was made and the tabernacle was raised, God showed up. We have the same principal at work today.

Raise God's Tabernacle

You may ask, "How are we going to raise a tabernacle? We don't have all that material. We don't have the plans He laid out for Moses. We don't have a requirement in the Bible to build a physical tabernacle." The apostle Paul made the point to the Corinthians that their bodies were the temple of God. (1 Cor. 3:16) Our bodies become that place where God will indwell, where God will meet with us and make His presence known to us.

So we still have to raise His tabernacle. We still have to sacrifice to build a suitable house where God can come in, be comfortable, and where His presence can be felt. If you want God to guide you then you are going to have to build His tabernacle. You're going to have to clean your house of all your old desires, clean your house of all your self will, and be able to present your body as a living sacrifice, holy, and acceptable unto Him. (Rom. 12:1) That is how you raise the tabernacle so that He can come in and dwell in you.

Put Jesus on the Throne

When you first received Jesus Christ as your Lord and Saviour, you didn't just get fire insurance. It's not just a matter of the Lord saving you from an eternal hell and forgiving your sins. You also have to do your part. You have to accept Him as Lord and Master—your King. You must receive Him as the one who is in charge of your life. When you receive Christ in that way and you allow Him to be the King on the throne of your heart, then you raise a tabernacle.

When we raise our tabernacle God shows up just like He

did for Israel. He will cover you with His cloud and with His fire. He will lead you and guide you in every step of your life. Then your job is simply to follow the cloud.

Everyone Moves at God's Command

Numbers 9:15-23 is one of the greatest sections in the Bible to learn about God's guidance and our obedience. Here we see how the Israelites faithfully kept the command of the Lord. *"The cloud was taken up from above the tabernacle, after that the children of Israel would journey. In the place where the cloud settled, there the children of Israel would pitch their tents. At the command of the Lord the children of Israel would journey and at the command of the Lord they would camp. As long as the cloud stayed above the tabernacle they remained in camp"* (Num. 9:17-18).

All the tribes had their tents in a circle around the tabernacle so the tabernacle stayed in the center of the nation. Then, when the cloud would begin to move away, they would pack up the tabernacle, pack up their tents, and begin to follow the cloud and move in that direction. They faithfully kept the command of the Lord, which meant they faithfully kept their eye on the cloud. Whenever it moved, they moved and whenever it stopped, they stopped.

What do you think would have happened if they ignored the cloud and stayed when the cloud moved off? What do you think would have happened if they kept walking when the cloud stopped? Sometimes you and I walk away from God and walk ahead of Him. Sometimes we lag behind. We don't move exactly when and where He's moving. God is a gracious God, but we need to understand that we are to obey Him. There's no promise that He's going to continue to guide us unless we are willing to obey His commands.

We must determine that when God says in His word, "Jump!"—our only question should be, "How high?" When God says, "Move!"—our only question should be, "In what direction?" We should be willing to faithfully keep His every command and keep our eye on that cloud. God is gracious but some of us are pushing His last nerve. We're at the edge of His tolerance table and we need to begin to obey God and follow the cloud. When it stops you stop. When it moves, you move. If God's Word says it then don't argue with it.

This is the kind of instant, unquestioned obedience that God wants from His people. It's not about what the preacher says or what the Church says. When God's Word says it, we need to obey and follow Him.

Who Is the Ultimate Authority?

There are few people who are at the place where they seek to obey God's every command. On one hand there are very few people who don't believe in God. Most people today believe there is a God in heaven somewhere. At the same time there are very few who will faithfully seek to follow Him. Most people don't even have God on the list of those with authority over them. I'm reminded of a story Cynthia Hulls tells in the Christian Reader about her 7 year-old son, with whom she and her husband were discussing being obedient to those in authority. She asked the little boy, "Who are some of the people who have authority over you in your life?" The 7 year-old started to think and said, "Well, you and Daddy and big sister when she is babysitting."

So the parents said, "Yes, that's right, if she's baby-sitting you she has authority. But who else has authority over you?" The boy said, "Well, at school, the teacher and principal and the cemeteries." That was a strange answer but they figured that since there was a cemetery near the schoolhouse, that's what he was referring to. The little boy corrected them and said, "No, the ladies in the office, the cemeteries, they have authority over me." That was a cute childish mistake but it illustrates a serious problem.

The bottom line for this 7 year-old is that God was not even on his list. And for many of us God is not on our list of those who have authority over us. If we are making our list in church in front of our brothers and sisters in the Lord, we will always put God on top, but what about away from the church? Who would top your list of authority figures in your life? You might list your employer. Many men would think of their wives, and women might list their husbands. But where does God come on your list of those you must follow? We know He belongs on top, yet for many He is far down the list. If you want God to guide you then you have to decide He is first of all to be obeyed.

Obedience is Life-giving

Resignation is the opposite of obedience. Resignation is surrender to faith but obedience is surrender to God. Elizabeth Elliot and her husband were missionaries in South America, called to share Christ with jungle tribesmen who had killed every missionary who ever tried to reach them with the Gospel. It was no different for her husband, Jim, who was murdered along with his co-workers. But Elizabeth went back to those very people and led many to Christ, including the man who killed her husband.

She says that, "Resignation lies down quietly in an empty universe and obedience rises up to meet God. Resignation says, "I can't" and obedience says, "I can." Resignation says, "It's all over for me", but obedience says, "Now that I'm here Lord, what's next?" Resignation says, "what a waste", and obedience asks, "Now Lord, what are you going to do with this mess?" This from a woman who lived out these words with great sacrifice and saw a harvest of souls.

We need to obey God. We need to know that God is leading us and guiding us. If we do, we will have a whole new attitude. Unlike the vast majority of people, we will live with the confidence of knowing that life is not totally dependent on our own wisdom and our own ability to make the right choices. We can be sure that God is leading and guiding in every situation.

Learning to Wait

The Israelites followed the Lord even when the cloud remained in one spot for a long time. *"Even when the cloud continued long, many days above the tabernacle, the children of Israel kept the charge of the Lord and did not journey"* (Num. 9:18). I can just imagine how the children of Israel were anxious to get to the land that God had promised. It was a land full of milk and honey! However, there was the cloud holding them back. It's not like they didn't know where the land of Canaan was. They knew but they stayed and obeyed.

Some of them must have been wondering, "Why does that cloud sometimes hang over the tabernacle for so many days and leave us stuck in one place for so long? Shouldn't we be moving on to the promised land?" If it were many of us today, we would just pack up our bags, hop in our cars and move on. We can be in such a hurry and sure that we know where we've got to go. But sometimes following God requires patience and staying under the cloud even when it's not moving anywhere.

Any parent who has a little boy can relate to this story. Recently, like many parents, I was getting my youngest son, Jason, a new glove for his little league team. Sometimes it takes more than one stop at a store and kids can get very impatient. We found a glove for $4.95. The little fellow was tired of all this shopping and he wanted to get it over with. Jason said, "Dad, buy me that one." But I said "No, that one will just rip up in a few weeks. I want to get something for you that's going to last." So he threw a little sulk session, not a major tantrum but the kind children do when they're impatient. He wanted his father to act quickly. But patience paid off and when we got to another store we found a $20 glove at half price and he got a good glove that lasted.

Following God and getting the good He has for us requires patience. We often want to jump ahead because we're anxious to get there and to accomplish things, but we need to learn to wait on the Lord. There are times that the cloud just seems to hang around and life seems to be at a standstill. We're not moving anywhere. But during these times, don't doubt that God has His purpose in our waiting. Whatever God's reason may be, if we're going to be obedient and be led by Him, we need to earnestly desire the ability to be patient.

Let me warn you to be prepared if you ask God to teach you patience. Roman 5:3 says, *"tribulation works patience."* To ask God for patience may be asking for God to allow some problems to come into your life that will teach you patience.

Always On the Move

Later in the story of the Israelites traveling through the wilderness we see the opposite problem occurring. *"And so it was, when the cloud remained only from evening until morning and when the cloud was taken up in the morning, then they would journey whether by day or by night. Whenever the cloud was taken up they would journey"* (Num. 9:21). There were days when the cloud only stayed overnight. It came in the evening and moved out in the morning.

Can you imagine being one of those Israelite families, trying to follow God and you don't know whether to pack or unpack? You get all unpacked and when you look out your tent in the morning you see you have to pack it up and move on. When following God there are days when there is no rest for the weary. There is no day off. Sometimes you get into one of those spells where you're just pushing and pushing. I think of my mother who followed my father around for so many years with all his traveling. It was often that way for her. He was home, then off again. She would unpack, throw a couple of things in the laundry, and throw it back in the bag, then off to the airport. It was often that way for her.

Many times following God requires that we don't get a whole lot of rest. In order to keep up with the cloud we can't lag behind God's leading. There are times when as soon as you lay your head down it's time to pack up and go. Jamie, a young adult at our church, talked about F.W.E.—"Functioning While Exhausted." We need to learn some F.W.E because the cloud doesn't always hang around. Sometimes God just keeps on moving and even when we are exhausted we need to keep up.

There are youth workers that give their all to run successful programs to help young people. There are missionaries that undergo hardships to evangelize the world. There are busy mothers that sacrifice to help out in Vacation Bible School. When we put forth that extra effort we may get so weary that our bedtime prayer will be "Lord, I am exhausted. Amen!" I think when we say that God smiles and makes sure we get a good night's rest.

Sometimes the cloud stays long and other times it just keeps on going. In either period we need to learn patience. In His sovereignty he regulates the pace of the cloud so that there is balance in our lives. We receive periods of rest when we need it but the resting time is also a time to get ready for when the cloud is moving. It's said that when the going gets easy you may be going downhill so try to find the balance. God honors it when you are obedient and you stick with His cloud.

Know Who You're Listening To

"At the command of the Lord they remained in camp and at the command of the Lord they journeyed. They kept the charge of the Lord, at the command of the Lord, by the hand of Moses" (Num. 9:23). They didn't play "Simon Says," they played, "The Lord Says." Do you remember how Simon Says works? You can only make a movement when the command begins with the words, "Simon says". If Simon doesn't say it, you don't do it, but if he does, you obey or you're out. It's the same way when you're following the Lord. We need to make sure that when the Lord says to move, we move. If the Lord doesn't say move and you're moving, you will soon find yourself without His guidance and out of His will.

The trick to winning in the game of Simon Says is to not get fooled by the logical flow of one movement following another. In other words, if you are in line with the others and the leader says, very quickly, "Simon says hands up! Hands down!" The tendency is to react to the second command automatically. Sometimes we get ahead of God because God says hands up and we think we have the next logical step figured out. So we go ahead and put our hands down even before God leads us and guides us into that step. The challenge is to follow the cloud and not race ahead or lag behind. In order to follow God's cloud, our human reason and logic have to be subordinated to His will and His direction in our lives.

Focusing Defies Reason

Just like winning in the game of Simon Says, if you're going to follow God you can't be influenced by what people next to you are doing, the movements they are making or the direction they're going in. Make sure that you focus on the cloud. When the cloud moves you follow the cloud and don't follow your neighbour. Don't just follow your deacons or your pastor. Many pastors get caught following the movements of other successful ministers rather than God's leading in their own life. Follow your pastors only as they follow the cloud because your first priority is to make sure that you're following that cloud.

Winning in the game of Simon Says also requires listening and focusing on what the person is saying. The way to win in Simon Says is to block everything out, all those other voices, and make sure that you're only listening to Simon. If you start listening to other voices you will get messed up. Our Christian walk is no different. We must block out all the other voices and determine to listen only to Him. As a follower of Christ are you determined to obey God no matter what the cost? Are you determined to study His Word for direction in your life and to follow it? Look inside and ask, "Is following the Lord, no matter where He leads me, my heart's greatest desire?

6
The Trumpets Signal What Time It Is

What time is it in America when Otto Nuss can highjack a school bus of kids from Berks County, Pennsylvania, and get them all the way down to Washington D.C. before the authorities catch up with him? What time is it in America when Michael Burgess in Ardmore, Pennsylvania, can blow away four of his family members and turn the gun on himself because of jealousy in his marriage and family? What time is it in America when teenagers in Norristown, Pennsylvania can go to school and be enticed by a security guard to make some extra money posing for lewd photos? I believe God is trying to open our eyes to the times we are in by speaking to us through such dramatic incidences in the world around us.

This is a time when so much can go so wrong so quickly. It's a time when your stock heavy pension plan can suddenly lose a third of its value and you don't know how you and your family will survive. It's a time when faithful employees working hard for the same company for twenty years can come to the office in the morning and find that they have been downsized or "rightsized" out of a job and pension and told to clear out their desk. It's a time when Jay, an Enron executive, sat in his Mercedes Benz by an exclusive housing development outside of Houston, Texas, in the midst of plush luxury, and because of all the chaos and financial uncertainty that surrounded him, took a gun and blew his brains out. For him, it was a time he could no longer bear to live in. What time is it for you?

God Wants to Lead You

God does not want us to be confused about the times we live in. He does not want us to be confused about where He wants us to go or what our next move should be. God's trumpet will signal to us exactly what time it is. In previous chapters we saw how the cloud was placed over the nation of Israel and they had the responsibility to move when the cloud moved. When the cloud stayed they were told to stay and when it moved, to move right along with the cloud and stay under its protection.

God hasn't changed. He is still in the business of alleviating any confusion about what He wants you to do. I can just imagine a regular guy, a "Joe Levi" in the nation of Israel, with bad cataracts and the inability to see when the cloud was moving on. Maybe he was lying down in bed when the cloud started to drift off. Joe, unable to see it, would be left behind. So God went one step further. Rather than just relying on their ability to keep track of the cloud, He decided to use trumpets as a means of communicating to His people. *"The Lord said to Moses: 'Make two trumpets of hammered silver, and use them for calling the community together and for having the camps set out'"* (Num. 10:1-2).

God is going to guide you whether you are ill or well; whether you are blind or can see. No matter what your situation is in life, He is there to lead you and to guide you. He is going to provide whatever is needed. If a cloud won't do it for you, if that doesn't get your attention, He's got a trumpet to blow in your ear as well. His guidance isn't hidden from us and God does not want His people to be confused.

God's Way of Leading

While the Nation of Israel was traveling through the wilderness they were led by the pillar of cloud and by the blowing of the trumpets. But when the Israelites got into the Promised Land, God kicked it up another notch. He communicated more specifically with the nation of Israel through the prophets. God used what we call the "major prophets" -- Isaiah, Jeremiah, Ezekiel and Daniel, to communicate to the Nation of Israel exactly what He wanted them to do.

In the same way that He raised the bar of guidance up a notch in the Promised Land, He has again increased communication in the church in the age in which we live. *"He communicated to us in a better way than the prophets. Now He has communicated to us through His Son, Jesus Christ, who is the express image of God. He is the brightness of His glory. He is the exact imprint of God"* (Heb.1:1-2).

If you want to know what God is like, just look to Jesus. If you want to know God's character and righteousness, just look to Jesus. If you want to know how much God loves you, where to go and the decisions you should make, just look to Jesus. He is the exact imprint of God the Father here on earth. God has chosen to communicate to us in a better way than He communicated with Israel. Today, we don't look to a cloud or to the prophets because God communicates to us directly through His Son, Jesus Christ. What a wonderful privilege we have today!

God Still Communicates

God went one step further in His desire to communicate with us. We don't have the advantage of being able to look to Jesus in person. We don't have the same advantage the disciples had when Jesus was walking and talking with them. Jesus knew He was going to ascend to the Father but He didn't want to leave us by ourselves, groping in the darkness or crawling around in our own wilderness. He wanted to alleviate the confusion so He promised to send us the Comforter, His Spirit, the Spirit of God.

First of all, the Spirit indwells us and guides us directly in our lives. The second thing the Spirit did was to move on Holy men of God to write down exactly what God wanted for us to learn. So today we have in our hands this book that we call the Bible. It's the revelation of God and His communication to us. It's better than a cloud or a trumpet. It's better than the earthly means that men use to guide them. It's better than the prophets of old. It is literally God's Word to us today. The Bible expresses

God's desire to eliminate the confusion in our lives and to communicate with us in a very specific way through His Word.

The Trumpet Gave The Signal To Gather

God used trumpets as a means of communicating to the nation of Israel in the wilderness. The trumpets would also signal when it was necessary to come together at the door of the Tabernacle. *"When they blow both of them all the congregation shall gather before you at the door of the Tabernacle of Meeting. But if they blow only one then the leaders, the head of the divisions of Israel shall gather to you"* (Num. 10:3-4).

God understood there would be times in the wilderness when they would be under attack. There were going to be times in the wilderness when sickness would be inside the tent and death would be knocking at the door. In the wilderness, money definitely couldn't buy happiness. There were no malls, movie theaters, television or the internet in the wilderness. There was nothing to distract them from the pain they suffered and the ills they went through.

There were times when they needed to gather together to provide strength for each other in order to provide the encouragement they needed. There were times when the Amelikites would come down with their army and attack. God knew there would be those moments when His people were going to have to come together, hold hands and group hug. That was the only way they were going to survive in that wilderness. They went through some good times and some bad times but God wanted them to know they needed to go through it together.

Iron Sharpens Iron, Faith Sharpens Faith

Going through the good and bad of life together is very critical for us today. The writer of Hebrews tells us that we need to make sure we *"don't forsake the assembling of ourselves together as is the custom of some"* (Heb. 10:25) Sometimes the trumpets blow because it's time for us to group hug. It blows today because it's time for us to come together and encourage each other. God understands that iron sharpens iron, and faith sharpens faith. That means if you have two knives and they rub up against each other, it will sharpen both blades. In the same way, your faith can strengthen my faith, my faith can strengthen yours, and when we gather together as a group, we are all strengthened.

There might be somebody who just crawled into church, head down, whose faith is dangling on a string. They barely plop into a pew and then someone shares a story of how God has blessed them and brought them through tough times. When one person's faith starts rubbing against another's and when stories are shared of how good God is, iron sharpens iron. It begins to register in a broken person's heart that if God did it for someone else, He can do it for him or her. If God is alive in somebody else's life then there's still hope for me in my circumstance. We can all leave church more encouraged in Jesus Christ. We might have crawled our way into church but we can skip and jump our way out. That's what God wants to do in our hearts.

We've Got to Help Each Other

You can't duplicate that kind of faith sharing experience sitting in front of a television. You can go up and down the dial but you can't sharpen anyone's faith watching TV. There are times when you can learn something from a TV or radio preacher, but that's no substitute for coming together. We live in a time that is getting so chaotic and crazy in this world that we must come together for strength and encouragement and to build each other up or we're just not going to make it.

Some people think they are super Christians, strong and faithful, but let me tell you it's not all about them. Maybe you're going through a phase in life where you think you're strong and you can get by without that group hug, but there will be others in the church that need it. Maybe they need to hear how God is working in your life. Maybe they need to rub up against your faith. It's not all about you. Getting together with other Christians is an act of obedience to God's Word, whether we feel we need it or not. We need to listen to the trumpet call that gathers us together and pulls us into the house of the Lord to strengthen and encourage each other.

You know what time it is? It's time for the church to gather together. The enemies of God are assembling and pooling their resources. They're strategizing. We as Christians need to make sure that we're pooling our resources and strategizing for the kingdom. We need to make sure that we're on the ball and doing what needs to be done so that the people of God can be built up and edified and not defeated by the devil and his helpers who are out to seek and destroy.

It's Time to Move

Not only was the trumpet used as a means of communication to call God's people together but Numbers 10:5-6 points out that the trumpet would signal when it was time to advance. *"When you sound the advance, the camps that lie on the east side shall then begin their journey. When you sound the advance the second time the camps that lie on the south side shall begin their journey. They shall sound the call to them to begin their journeys."* When the trumpet sounded and the cloud began to move away from over the tabernacle it was time for the nation to pack up and to move forward. There are times when the trumpet blows in our lives and it's time for us to advance.

As the cloud moved away from over the tabernacle, naturally the priests were the first ones who noticed and they had the responsibility to blow the trumpet. God didn't have 100 trumpets blowing all over the camp. Today, God has given some people in the church the responsibility to keep their eye on the cloud. It's the responsibility of God appointed leaders to see to it that they don't' get distracted by all the things going on in the world.

All the issues we face of making a living can keep us from watching the cloud. Surely there were people in the camp who, because of their occupation, were out of sight of the tabernacle. Some were sick in their tents and unable to see the tabernacle and the cloud. They couldn't be expected to sound the alarm because they couldn't keep their eyes on the cloud. But the priests had the responsibility of knowing when the cloud was moving and sounding the trumpet and in the church today, we have leaders who have that responsibility. We need to respect them and to listen when they tell us it's time to pack up and move so we can determine if the cloud is moving for us.

We Each Have a Responsibility

While it was the responsibility of the priest to blow the trumpet and to tell everybody it was time to advance, it was also each individual Israelite's responsibility to know where the cloud was. Everyone had their work in the camp just as we have our occupations today, but they still had to keep an eye on the cloud. Their final confirmation that it was time to move didn't come just from the trumpet. They would look at the cloud. That is critical because some people think that whatever the preacher says and whatever the church comes out with, that's what they're going to roll with.

But each one of us as believers has access to see the cloud. We have God's communication right here in the Bible. If the preacher comes out and tells you some crazy thing that is absolutely out of line with God's Word, there should be Christians knocking him over to say that the cloud isn't going there. Every one of us has that responsibility. If the cloud is moving you should be able to look with your own two eyes and see whether or not the cloud is moving. When it is, and it's time for you to move, you have that final responsibility.

God Is the Ultimate Guide

Sure, God raises up men who have dedicated years to the study of His Word. Sure, God uses them to give us insight into what He is doing and what God is saying in our lives. But the final responsibility rests with each one of us to get into our own Bibles and get into our own prayer closets to check out the cloud for ourselves and find out what God is doing.

There is a well-known psychiatrist who recently wrote a book about how life is shaped by five key relationships, seven major decisions, and 10 opportunities. In other words he's saying there are just a few critical choices, events, and people in your life that shape your whole existence. There are a few key decisions that will drastically alter the parameters of your life. When those opportunities come you need to be in touch with what God wants you to do. Just one wrong turn in one key decision can change your life forever and you can't back track and do it over again.

Offering or saying yes to that one wrong marriage proposal can throw your whole life into a whirlwind. Innocently saying yes to that one seemingly great job opportunity when that's not what God wants you to do can change your whole life. Missing an opportunity from God because He is pulling you in one direction but you want to go in another can have disastrous and lifelong results.

We need to make sure that whatever else we do in our lives, we keep an eye on the cloud. Today we have a clear sound of one trumpet blowing. We have a clear sound of God speaking in His Word. We have a clear sound of the Spirit of God as He impresses Himself on our hearts. Stay in touch with that trumpet and Word and simply obey. Have no fear. God won't lead you down the wrong path.

The problem for so many Christians is that they have the TV turned up so loud, the radio blasting and the CD playing that the still small trumpet sound of God is not being heard. On a daily basis we need to turn off all those other distractions. On a daily basis we need to get alone with God in that quiet place, open up to Him and have Him speak to us through His Word. On a daily basis we need to open up our hearts to the voice of His Spirit and let Him lead us and guide us through life.

God doesn't want to confuse you, He wants to lead and guide you. He wants to eliminate all the confusion. If the cloud is moving away and the trumpet is blowing, the kingdom of God suffers if you don't go. Ministries go unfilled if you don't go. You'll never be able to find fulfillment in your life if you don't go when the cloud says go. If you don't go when the trumpet sounds you're going to miss some of those key opportunities in your life.

Protection from the Enemy

The trumpet would also signal when the enemy was coming. *"The trumpet would signal. When you go to war in your land against the enemy who oppresses you. Then you should sound the alarm with the trumpets. And you will be remembered before the Lord your God. And you will be saved from your enemies"* (Num. 10:9) What a wonderful thing to be remembered before the Lord, to

THE TRUMPETS SIGNAL WHAT TIME IT IS

have God with you, watching over you, caring about you and remembering you. The trumpets sounded an alarm when the enemy was coming. If today, you will follow Him and heed His alarm, God will always be there for you. He'll remember you and see you through.

The Bible warns us about relying on our own understanding. We're warned about the problem sin has created and that there is an enemy out to destroy us. We're warned to not neglect the great salvation God has provided. The Bible is full of warnings for us and it's our job to heed them. Are you paying attention to the warnings of God?

Sometimes the way we deal with God is the way we deal with the alarm clock next to our beds. When it goes off in the morning we roll over, hit the snooze button and tell it to get back to us in ten minutes. God comes and alarms us again and we say, "Lord, I know you're right but get back to me in a few months." But God never gives up on us and when He comes again, some of us hit the snooze button again and say, "God, why don't you get back to me in a couple of years." Have you ever done that?

In your daily life you can hit that snooze button and get another 10 minutes sleep, but your employer isn't pushing back your punch-in time 10 minutes on the other end. You still have to show up at work on time. You may have some flexibility on your end to play the snooze game, but on the other end he's going to start docking your pay if you show up late.

We need to understand that God is just like that. When God is trying to get your attention and He's got the trumpets blowing, one in each ear, His timetable is fixed and He is not moving His obligations on the other side. He is still expecting what He's expecting and you need to start obeying Him right now. Today is the day of salvation. When His alarm is going off, don't try to "snooze" God. You better jump up and start doing what He has commanded you to do. When the cloud starts moving away it's time to advance. God's got a mission for you and it's not the time to roll over in bed. It's not time to spend another few months or weeks or even days being disobedient. It's time to start obeying God.

God wants you to know that He loves you. He wants you to experience His wonderful plan for your life. But He knows there is an enemy seeking whom he can devour and he's out to destroy you 24/7. You have to pay attention to God's alarm system or you're not going to make it. He will bring you to safety and accomplish that wonderful plan in your life but you've got to obey. That's your part of the deal and it's not optional.

The Rewards of Obedience

Notice what happened when the nation of Israel was in the wilderness and they obeyed the alarm. They were remembered before the Lord. What would happen in the church today if we came together after each of us lifted God up in our lives and put Him on the throne of our hearts? How would that change us when we gathered together? Don't you see what the Lord could do in our communities if He had Christians who would make a total commitment to Him? As a pastor, that's my dream and vision for the church, but it's only going to happen as men and women turn to Jesus and begin to obey Him and to execute God's plan for their lives. It will happen when they realize the gifts and abilities God has given them and they begin to commit that to God.

It starts with you. Don't snooze God anymore. Don't roll over and push Him aside anymore. It starts in obedience today, right now, making a fresh commitment to Him. Tell Him, "Lord, if you say move, I want to move. If you say wait, I want to wait. I want to do whatever you want me to do."

If you will simply trust in Jesus, He will always remember you and He will never, never leave you. Obey Him and He guarantees you the victory. Listen to His trumpet sound and He will direct your paths. Worship Him with your life, study His Word and put Him on the throne of your heart. Experience the victory of being in the centre of His will and His presence will never leave you.

7
God Is In the Drivers Seat

A father stood dismayed in the middle of the kitchen in his family's home while in the process of doing some renovating. His wife had given him the job of painting the kitchen country orange. The pan of paint was in the middle of the floor and as he was busily working he plunked his left foot right into the paint. He pulled out his soggy foot and wished he had brought another pair of socks he could change into. He had to leave the house with orange toes showing through his open-toe sandals.

That wouldn't be too bad except that he had to pick up his kids from the baby sitter before going back home. When he got to the sitter's home his kids were still napping. The baby sitter suggested that rather than the father waking up his kids that he go take care of some business, maybe buy a pair of socks and come back later. He thought of a million things he could do with the free time and he headed toward the mall.

On the way to the mall he remembered that he had orange toes sticking out of his sandals, but being the secure man that he was, he didn't let the thought of traipsing through the mall that way put a stop to his shopping and he headed for the housewares section. As he was picking up some accessory items and choosing colors, he realized that the accident was a blessing in disguise since he was able to match his country orange socks to some of the things he wanted to pick up for the kitchen.

God Cares about the Details

It may seem like a stretch to believe that God had His hand in that. There are people who will tell us that God is too busy running the universe to be concerned about the tiny details of our lives. But God is always in the driver's seat and even in the most minute details of our lives, God is right there with us, concerned about us and wanting to "work all things together for good."

That is also the point of the stories in Numbers Chapter 11. They tell us that God is always in the driver's seat. Whether we face big problems or small, God is in charge. This should be an encouragement to Christians as we look at the situations we wrestle with in our own lives. God is there, sitting on the throne and He is always in charge.

God Dictates His Own Terms

First notice that God responds on His own terms. He is not limited by what you and I think. *"So Moses went out and told the people the words of the Lord. And he gathered the 70 men of the elders of the people and placed them around the tabernacle. Then the Lord came down in the cloud and spoke to him and took of the Spirit that was upon him and placed the same upon the 70 elders; and it happened when the Spirit rested upon them that they prophesied although they never did so again"* (Num. 11: 24-26). God responded on His own terms and He gave the Spirit of God to these 70 men based on His own desires.

The people had been complaining because all they had to eat was manna. They didn't have all the good food that they enjoyed in Egypt. They thought about all the vegetables, herbs, spices, and meat they used to enjoy eating in Egypt. Now, morning after morning, day after day, week after week, they stepped out of their tents to face the same old manna. So they started to complain.

Not only did the people complain to Moses, but Moses, that great leader, turned around and started complaining to the Lord. In Numbers 11:10-15, Moses basically said, "Lord, you have to do something about these people. What did I do to You to deserve having to carry around this bunch of crybabies? How can I lead two million Israelites when all they do is complain." In fact, Moses' distress with the Israelites is the closest thing to a suicide note that we have in the Bible. In verse 15 he says, *"Lord, if I've done anything to please you, just put me to death! I'd rather check out than having to continue to lead this crew!"*

So the Lord gave him an answer. He told Moses to pick out 70 men and tell them to surround the tabernacle and that His Spirit would come down upon them and after they would share the burden of caring for the people along with Moses. Notice what happened. Moses pulled out a paper and pen and made a list of 70 men he thought were faithful, qualified, and able to help him. Then he invited those 70 men to come around the tabernacle. The Bible tells us that all but two of the 70 surrounded the tabernacle. Eldad and Medad didn't go. They were still in the camp. Maybe they got up late, their alarm didn't go off, or breakfast was running long. Whatever the reason, they were still in the camp and they weren't where they were supposed to be.

God Meets Us Where We Are

You might think these two elders would be in big trouble, but the Bible tells us that the Spirit of God fell upon them even though they didn't show up where they were commanded to be. *"But the two men had remained in the camp. The name of one was Eldad, the name of the other was Medad and the Spirit rested upon them. Now they were among those listed but not among those who had gone out into the tabernacle"* (Num. 11:26) Even though they missed a meeting with Moses and the greatest leaders among all the people and the promise to be touched by the very Spirit of God, the Lord still poured His Spirit upon them!

I am so glad that God uses us even when we fail. Even when we are not where we are supposed to be or doing what we're supposed to be doing, He will use us. That may not mean a lot to you if you are one of those people who is always in the right place at the right time, but for the rest of us I'm glad God is gracious and merciful. He responds with mercy and on His own terms and not by our standards.

The Perfect World

Recently, I was with some cadets that I chaplain in the Civil Air Patrol at the Willow Grove Navel Base, in Willow Grove, PA. These are teenagers, 13 to 18 years old, and most of them have never been to church. They don't have a clue who Jesus is. About once a month I do what the Civil Air Patrol calls, "moral leadership". That's my opportunity to get them to think about the Gospel. We have what are supposed to be non-denominational type discussions to get them to think about moral character.

During one of the sessions I told them to break up into small groups and create a world that would be a great place to live. Then come back and describe that world to the rest of the group. They were to tell us what it looks like, feels like, etc. When they reported on their ideal worlds, some of them had really creative ideas. One group had a world with nothing but tropical islands. Everything was sunshine and beauty all the time. Another group had a biodome where the environment was controlled and there were no extremes in the weather.

Then I told them to go back into their small groups and tell me about the people living in these worlds and how they interacted with each other. Of course they came up with things like, "everybody loves everybody" or "everybody cares about everybody" or "everyone respects each other". There were all sorts of utopian ideas. I then sent them back into the small group and asked what rules they were going to have so that nobody would come into their wonderful world and mess it up. If you want a place where everybody loves and respects each other then what are you going to do if somebody violates that? What happens if somebody breaks into someone else's house and steals or does violence to another person? What rules are you going to enforce so you maintain a wonderful place to live? They came back with a list of rules and many of them sounded just like the 10 Commandments.

I sent them back one more time and told them to think about what the punishment would be if someone violated these rules. Every single one of the six groups, without exception, came back with a policy of no mercy, no grace, no second chances. One group said that if somebody violated a rule they would be put on a space ship and sent off into space. Another group had a militia team ready so that when someone violated the rules he or she would just be killed. They didn't talk about a court system. There were no appeals. If you got caught; that was it; you were just blown away.

God's Enduring Mercy

I thank God that He doesn't respond to us the way we would like to respond to each other. Sometimes, we don't have a whole lot of patience for each other. We don't always have a lot of grace. Many times we would like God to throw the hammer down on somebody else, but God responds on His own terms. He is in the driver's seat. He's in charge. He is the One that is gracious and merciful. He is the One that always cares about us. What a tremendous thing it is that we deal with a gracious God.

"Then Peter came to Him and said, 'Lord, how often shall my brother sin against me, and I forgive him? Up to seven times?' Jesus said to him, 'I do not say to you, up to seven times, but up to seventy times seven'" (Matt. 18:21-22) Unlimited forgiveness was Jesus' answer, and when we look at Jesus we are looking at the human embodiment of God and His attitude toward us.

We may spit in God's face and turn our back on Him. We may tell Him, "God, I don't want to have anything to do with you!" And in the face of our rebellion He is still blessing us, loving us, having mercy on us, giving us His air to breath, food to eat, shoes on our feet, and houses to live in. God responds differently than I would and I thank Him for His grace and mercy.

God Knows What We Need

But God also provides based on His own terms. To put this fact in context is to remember that the Israelites were complaining because they only had manna to eat. They wanted something more. They wanted meat. So God said, "You want meat to eat, I'll give you some meat!" Numbers 11:31-32 says, *"Now a wind went out from the Lord and it brought quail from the sea and left them fluttering near the camp. About a day's journey on this side and about a day's journey on the other side, all around the camp and about two cubits above the surface of the ground. And the people stayed up all that day and night. And all the next day and gathered the quail. He who gathered the least gathered 10 homers and they spread them out for themselves all around the camp."*

The people had complained about not having any food so God provided food in a miraculous way. This was not a normal flock of quail flying by and the Israelites shot down a few to get some meat. This was nothing they could simply explain away as a natural phenomenon. It was clearly the hand of God that sent a wind that drove the quail into the camp. There was more quail than they had ever seen before and more than they could ever even dream about. There was quail coming in the sky as high as the eye could see.

In terms of quantity, the homer is about 60 gallons. The most decrepit, arthritic person, who walked with a walker and could hardly bend down to pick a quail off the ground, picked up 10 homers. That's about 600 gallons of quail. "You want quail?" God said, "I'll give you some quail!" In a miraculous way God provided more meat than they could even think about. He provided based on His own terms.

God had a reason why He gave them that much. He wanted them to learn a lesson. The important thing for us to understand is that just because God provides abundance does not mean God is showing approval. Sometimes God gives us abundance because He wants to teach us something. There are some lessons you can't learn unless you have some difficulties to deal with in your life. There are some things that being poor you'll never learn. There are other things that being rich you'll never learn. God provided the quail in a way to teach the Israelites that lesson.

Stop and think about this. All day long and all night long and all the next day they were up gathering quail. It so clearly shows that there was a lack of faith in God's provision. Before there was quail, God showed them with the manna that He was there every day for them. Every morning there was manna enough to eat and all they had to do was gather what they needed for that one day and there would be manna again the next day. But they got fed up with the manna and so God sent all these quail.

Why couldn't they trust God that if they just picked up a few quail to feed their family for that day, God would provide more for them the next day? But their greed showed a lack of trust and a lack of faith in God. Their greed took over and everything they could get their hands on they wanted to stick in their pockets. They didn't trust God further than they could see.

Before we criticize them let's think about ourselves. Many of us don't trust God for tomorrow. We don't trust God for next year. We want to stick it in our pockets right now. If it's not in my pocket, not in my safe, if I can't see it or it's not on my bank statement, then I can't believe God for it. Many can't even bring themselves to tithe. We need to come to the place where we recognize that God has promised to meet our needs.

God is still going to be there for us tomorrow and next week and for the rest of our lives. I might not have what I think I need for next week but I'm still going to have Jesus next week. I might have more month than money but I know that God's going to be there for me at the end of the month. God's going to see you through. We need to learn to trust God. We need to learn to rely on Him and not always hoard for ourselves out of a lack of faith.

Notice what happened with the Israelites. They were so selfish and untrusting of God that they stored up more quail than they could possibly eat. It had to have dawned on somebody that there was no refrigerator to stick it in. All they could see was the food in front of their faces and they were determined to store up as much quail as they could. It is absolutely bizarre how people can be taken over by greed.

Trust God

One of the things God's miraculous provision to the Israelites teaches us is that we should never put a limitation in our minds on what God can do. When you reach those spells in your life when you think there's nothing else God can do, guess what, God is able to come through and come through in abundance. He is able to do much more than we can ever ask or think. Don't ever get tired of praying for that husband or wife or a lost and troubled teenager. Don't ever get tired of praying for that close friend or relative. There are no cases that are too tough for God. There are no cases that are hopeless or too far-gone. God is always able to come through and He is in charge.

You can't dig yourself into a financial hole that's too deep for God to pull you back out. You can't be so sick that God can't restore you back to health. There is no family difficulty that is so dysfunctional that God can't interject His hand and make a difference. So don't give up trusting and never give up praying about it. Keep relying on God. He is able to provide. Don't complain about the circumstance you're in. Don't complain about what God hasn't done. Trust God for what He can do and what He's able to do in your life and God will never let you down. Just remember that God doesn't feel the time pressure of your life span. God provides for us based on His own terms from an eternal perspective.

Don't Be Discouraged

It's encouraging as we go down our little prayer lists when we can check off a God-answered prayer. It is a tremendous lift to our faith when God answers our prayers in a miraculous way. But there are other things on our prayer lists that are carried over from page to page, month to month, and year to year. We've been praying for those same things for years and years and still, there they are on our prayer list. It's easy sometimes to get discouraged that God is not working. It's easy for us to feel let down by God and to have our faith begin to wane. But remember that God is still in the driver's seat. He's the one driving this bus and He will see to it that our needs are met. He provides on His own terms. Somebody once said, "God provides not when you want it, but it's always on time."

God's Holy Wrath

God's anger is also aroused on His own terms. *"While the meat was still between their teeth, before it was chewed, the wrath of the Lord was aroused against the people. And the Lord struck the people with a very great plague"* (Num. 11:33). Imagine the scene; the Israelites, hungry for meat, are gorging themselves with quail and it's just hanging out of their mouths. God is getting angrier and angrier because they don't trust Him. After all He has done for them and how He has provided, still their faith isn't in Him and they are greedy and selfish and thinking only about themselves.

Imagine that I invited you over to my house for dinner and my wife, Carol, puts out a spread of food on the table. Since you're the guest I tell you to go first and help yourself. You grab a big plate and start scooping huge mounds of food onto your plate. I mutter under my breath, "I've got my kids and they need to eat too, save something for people behind you." But you're the guest in the house, so I don't want to say anything. But there you are, a guest in my home, piling food on your plate and basically disrespecting my family and not caring about anybody else but yourself. As your plate is being stacked high with everyone's food the anger of the host is rising too.

That's a similar situation to the plight of the selfish Israelites. God was blessing them, answering their prayers, meeting their needs, but instead of seeing God, instead of trusting God, all they could see were piles of food in front of them. If there were more space on the plate they would stick in another helping of food. It would be almost as if I told Carol, "You know what? If our guest wants food we'll give him food! Stick another chicken in the oven and put another pot of rice on the stove! We will pile the food in front of him and make him eat it until he gets really sick!"

And that's what I believe God did to teach the Israelites the lesson of knowing that He is able to meet their needs. He is able to provide, even miraculously. But He also challenged them about their selfishness and lack of faith and trust. God's huge supply of quail turned out to be a judgement against these people and their lack of faith.

God's Anger Is Unique

God's anger is interesting because anger is one of the things we all can identify with. It's one of those areas where, being created in His image, we can share that with Him. But God gets angry on His own terms and He doesn't get angry like we get angry. God gets angry at sin. God gets angry at unfaithfulness. God gets angry at our selfishness. But a different list of aggravations angers us.

I think about the man who spent three and a half hours at the department of motor vehicles. During this time he put up with insane regulations, surly clerks, bad attitudes, and all the stuff you run into in the worst of bureaucracy. After three and a half hours, understandably, he had a pretty bad attitude. On his way home he remembered he had to pick up a toy for his son. So he stopped at the toy store and found a baseball bat that would make the perfect gift.

He took the bat to the checkout counter and the cashier asked if he would be paying by cash or charge. He shouted back, "Cash!" Then he caught himself because he realized that He was acting like he was still back at the DMV. He apologized to the cashier and told her that he really didn't mean to snap at her like that. He explained, "I just came from the department of motor vehicles and put up with all kinds of nonsense. I didn't mean to take it out on you." The cashier took the bat in hand and asked, "Well, do you want me to gift wrap it or are you going back to the DMV?"

We can all identify with the anger this man had. But God doesn't get angry with the DMV. God is not angry at the situations that frustrate us in life. God is angry at our unbelief. He's angered by those times when He tells us what we should do and we do something else. He's angry when He demonstrates His love to us and we put blinders on and pretend that He doesn't exist. He's angry when we choose to live life as though He is not even around. That makes Him angry.

God is angry at our sin because all sin is ultimately against Him. In Psalm 51, David writes of his realization, *"Against thee and thee only have I sinned."* If I tell you a lie, I should apologize to you for telling you the lie, but ultimately I've got to deal with God because all sin is against Him. The Bible teaches us that it's a fearful thing to fall into the hands of an angry God, and God gets angry on His own terms and in His own time.

God Anoints As He Sees Fit

In the story about Eldad and Medad we see that God anointed on His own terms. These two men remained in the camp and the Spirit rested upon them. They were among those listed that had not gone out to the tabernacle, yet they prophesied in the camp. *"And the young man ran and told Moses and said, "'Eldad and Medad are prophesying in the camp.' So Joshua, the son of Nun, Moses' assistant, one of His choice men, answered and said. 'Moses, my Lord, forbid them'"* (Num. 11: 26-28). In other words, Joshua wanted to stop them from prophesying. If they were not doing what Joshua thought they were supposed to be doing, and if they were not where they were supposed to be, Joshua wanted them stopped.

But Moses told Joshua, *"Are you zealous for my sake? I wish that all the Lord's people were prophets and that the Lord would put His Spirit upon them,"* Then Moses and the elders of Israel returned to the camp. (Num. 11:29-30) Moses came to grips with the fact that God anoints on His own terms. It's not based on Moses' desires, likes, dislikes, opinion, or assessment of the situation. God does what He wants to do, and He enables people and gifts people based on what His desires are for His own purposes and reasons.

God is in Charge

This story has a lot of important application in the church. In the church, God is in charge. If you thought that your pastor was in charge you were misled. He is not in charge of the church and the elders and deacons are not in charge. God is in charge of the church. He's the one who dictates to us what it is that we are supposed to do. One of the ways He tells us is by bringing certain gifts into the church.

We don't go to God and tell Him, "We need to have this program or we need to have that program." And then we start trying to fill those needs with the people that we have. That leads to squeezing round pegs into square holes. Leaders often put people in areas where they are not really gifted just to fill a need and to keep a program going. But who said that you've got to have a teen group? Who said that you've got to have children's ministry? Who said that you have to have a choir? And who said that any of those ministries are indispensable? God is the one who's in charge and He tells us what ministries we should have by the gifts He brings into the church. If there is any ministry that a church should have, we'll know because God will provide the gifts for us to operate that ministry.

If I (or any pastor) come up with an idea for a ministry and I call people up and say we need this or we need that, and the church desperately needs your help, please come." If that's not an area where someone is gifted then a problem will develop because people are being squeezed into areas of ministry God never intended them to be. It is our job, as Ephesians 4 says, to equip the saints for the work of ministry.

My job as pastor is not to define or create the ministry, but to equip the saints to help discover where God wants them to be. My job is to do all I can to give them all they need so that they can operate that ministry and see it come to fruition for the church. The point is, God is in the driver's seat and He will lead His church. We just need to be sensitive as a church to the leading of the Holy Spirit telling us where we should be going and what we shouldn't be doing by His operation of the gifts inside the church. The church is not to be led by the creative thinking of the pastor or by the elders in some elders meeting, unless that creative idea comes from and is gifted by God. I believe this kind of sensitivity to the Holy Spirit is the winning formula for any church.

God's Unique Plan For Us

Not only does this method of decision making have implication for the church, but it also has implication for each one of us individually. In the very same way we understand that God anoints on His terms for the church, He also anoints and gives gifts to each one of us on His own terms. For example, as much as I like music, He didn't give me the ability to sing. My sisters can sing but that ability just skipped right over me. God, for His own reasons, knew where He wanted me to fit into the body. It's my job to figure out how God has gifted me and how I am supposed to fit into the body. If He didn't make me a singer then someone else is supposed to lead the singing.

Another example is with little children. I don't have the patience, like some people do, to have two and three-year-olds running around my knees, chasing me around the nursery. I don't have the patience to read little nursery stories to children while some are crying and others are fidgeting and crawling around. I couldn't do it. But I praise God that He has given some people in the church the patience and even the joy to be able to do that.

You see, when all of us come together, with the gifts the Spirit has given to us, we have an array of spiritual gifts available.

Then you see the flourishing of a multitude of ministries to work His purpose out in each one of our lives. If each one of us recognizes that God is in charge and that He anoints and enables us based on His own terms and purposes, then we need to submit ourselves to God's will. Each one of us, like the hymn writer says, needs to come to God and say, "Have Thine own way Lord, have Thine own way. Thou art the Potter, I am the clay."

It's amazing that God will use us even though we are not always where we're supposed to be. It's amazing that God will still allow His Spirit to fall down on us even when we're not always found around the tabernacle like we're supposed to be. God is pleased when He sees the saints in the church consecrate their lives to Him and say, "Lord, You enable me. You work it out in my life and You anoint me with your Spirit. Let your Spirit fall down on me and let me do what it is You want me to do." God is a good God. He's a gracious and loving God. He wants to use us and He cares about each one of us. He enables us and gifts us. He anoints us according to His own terms. It doesn't always make sense to us but if each one of us will allow God to work it out in our own lives, what a ministry we would see.

8
Bear Up Under the Pressure

One thing we all experience is stress. Some go through more challenges and trials than others but we all experience our fair share of stress. As we take a look at the children of Israel and their progress in the wilderness on their way to the promised land, we find steps that can enable us to bear up. These principles can help you deal successfully with financial, family, work or any other kind of stress.

Moses Was Stressed Out

When we look at Moses' situation we find that he was under a lot of stress. He said to God *"Where am I to get meat to give all these people? For they weep all over me saying give us meat that we may eat. I am not able to bear all these people alone because the burden is too heavy for me"* (Num. 11:13-14) Now, just for a moment, put yourself in Moses' shoes. He has to lead six hundred thousand men, and if we include the women and children, it is estimated that there were at least 2 million people walking through the wilderness with God feeding them manna from heaven.

Every morning they would go out, pick up the manna and bring it in to eat. When your food is free and drops from heaven every day, you thank the Lord. You'd certainly thank the Lord the first week, maybe even for the first month, but imagine, day in and day out, month after month, manna for breakfast, manna for lunch and manna for dinner. Even if it were especially delicious, after a while you would get sick of seeing the same meal. So the Israelites started to complain to Moses that they wanted some meat to eat. They remembered the variety of things they were used to eating in Egypt.

Moses felt helpless and was going through a lot of stress, and not just about manna. This also caused people to question his leadership ability. How in the world was he going to provide meat for this group of two million people in the wilderness? He didn't even provide the manna. Food from heaven is a God thing, not a leadership decision. It was just too much for him to bear. He told the Lord that if He didn't solve this problem it would be better for him to die. I think we can identify with Moses. I'd rather give up and throw in the towel than bear pressure from two million people without any kind of solution.

Stress Principles to Live By

Unless you are a world leader, you don't have 2 million people to feed every day. Your pressures are different. Maybe you have two little mouths quacking at the table and you're under pressure to bring home the bacon. Maybe you've got a stack of bills and people calling and asking when they will get paid. Maybe you've got a spouse who looks at you and remembers the dreamer he or she married and all the promises you made when you got married that aren't even close to being fulfilled. That happens to Christians, too. All of us face a variety of pressures in our lives and they come at us from different directions. But the end result is that we as believers need to understand that God gives us some principles so that we can rise up above the stress and earthly circumstances.

Share the Burden with Others

Here is the first principle we can take from Moses situation with the Israelites as found in Numbers 11:16. *"So the Lord said to Moses, gather to me 70 men of the elders of Israel, who you know to be the elders of the people. And officers over them bring them to the tabernacle of meeting, that they may stand there with you."* The lesson here is that we are to join hands with the rest of the body so that we can all work together to bear up under the pressure. Essentially, God was telling Moses, "Don't try to bear it all yourself. Get some help. Gather some wise and able people around you and let them share the load. Don't be a lone ranger."

Some people have told me that I can be like a lone ranger. Sometimes I go out and start doing and don't always bring the whole crew with me. That's a bad attribute for any of us to have. We're not to go out and try to face the enemy and fight the battles on our own. The pressure is going to be too much for us.

We are a part of the body of Christ. Romans 12 and 1st Corinthians 12 tells us that the body of Christ is made up of a lot of different members. Some of us are hands, some are ears, some feet, some eyes and some heads and we are all essential and all have different roles that we play in the body. The body needs all of us functioning together in order to operate properly. If you ask your little finger to carry the whole load without the help of all the fingers then it would be too much for that little finger to carry. But all working together can manage all that God allows to come at us as we travel through life.

At our church, Montco Bible Fellowship, God has blessed us with some good brothers and sisters and we take advantage of each other to help carry the burdens. It's not God's way to try to face the stress and the pressures of life alone. Take advantage of each other! There are those in the church who are not only willing to carry the burden along with you, they want to. Jesus said that He came not to be served but to serve, and to give His life as a ransom for many. Let's be like Jesus.

At the Lake Elementary School in Ocean Side, California, Mr. Alters 5th grade class had 14 boys who were all bald. They all shaved their heads, even though only one of the boys needed to. His name was Ian and he had cancer. When he went through chemotherapy his hair fell out in clumps. His parents decided to shave his head so that he would at least have a uniform look. Ian's friend, Kyle, gathered the other guys together and decided that in order to make Ian feel better they would all shave their heads so nobody would single out the one who had cancer and Ian could blend in with the rest of the group.

That's a practical and inspiring example of how to carry someone's burden. We're not so naïve or ignorant that we can't do a little creative thinking amongst ourselves and come up with ways to help carry one another's burdens. The issue is really a love and a heart issue. Do we really care about the problems that other people face and the stress they are carrying? Or do we just plop ourselves in front of our big-screen digital TV all evening when our brothers and sisters are struggling alone out there? It's a heart issue that we need to challenge ourselves about.

Galatians 6:2 says, *"Carry each other's burdens and in this way you fulfill the law of Christ."* Don't be a lone ranger. Share your burdens with others and the rest of us as a part of the body of Christ need to be willing to pick up the slack. We need to be willing to make sacrifices for each other and carry a little of the burden. It all boils down to the great commandment. Jesus said that if you love God and you learn to love your neighbour as yourself you fulfill all the law and the prophets. Stress management in the body of Christ comes down to sharing our burdens with those Godly people that God has put into our lives to help us carry the burden. To turn them away is actually an act of disobedience.

Jesus Can Meet All Our Needs

When we help people we need to point them to God because ultimately, only God can meet their deepest needs. *"Then I will come down and talk with you there. I will take up the Spirit that is upon you. I will put the same upon them and they shall bear the burdens of the people with you that you may not bear it yourself, alone"* (Num. 11:17). People in and of their own strength can't help that much. They were starving before God brought the manna and they certainly couldn't come up with the meat they desired. All of them working together couldn't solve the problems they were facing. As Moses gathered the elders around he laid hands on them and God promised to work through Moses' appointment and supply to those men the same Spirit of God that Moses experienced in his life.

There's a very important lesson here because so many times we get the feeling we are the only ones who can do it and nobody else can do it like we can. That's just human nature but it doesn't serve the will of God. He promises that if we gather the body of Christ around us and delegate others to carry out the work, the same Spirit of God who enables us can enable them and can work through them. We need to take advantage of that if we want

God's promise to work through the body to be fulfilled.

The Lord then told Moses, *"Then you shall say to the people consecrate yourselves for tomorrow. And you shall eat meat, for you have wept in the hearing of the Lord saying 'who will give us meat to eat? For it was well with us in Egypt.' Therefore the Lord your God will give you meat and you shall eat"* (Num. 11:18) You see, God didn't say to Moses that he was going to be able to come up with the meat. He didn't say to the 70 elders, "You 70, you're going to be able to solve this problem." But what He did say was that the Lord your God is going to supply the need.

Our desire should be to get to the place in our lives where we understand and accept that some situations are way over our heads. There are some problems that are in our families that we can never solve. There are some relatives that we can argue with until the cows come home, and we're blue in the face and it will never make a difference. There are some people and some circumstances on the job that you in your own power will never be able to make a difference. But God says that in order to bear up under the stress, remember that He can meet your need and change your circumstances and make the difference.

So we point people to Jesus. Don't take all the responsibility on yourself. Don't always tell people that you're going to do something for them when maybe what they need is for you to point them to Jesus. The more you have people looking toward you and relying on you to come up with answers and solutions in their lives, the more you realize that you better reflect and deflect all that attention and point people to Jesus.

When people come into my office and want answers to their problems and want circumstances changed in their lives, it would be crazy for me to take that responsibility on as though I can make the difference. The best thing I can do is point them to Jesus because He alone is the one who changes people's lives and makes the ultimate difference. It's just pride that makes us prop ourselves up in to a position where we try to be the solution. We need to repent and turn people over to Jesus.

God the Provider

Moses came to understand that God is the one who could

supply all of their needs. If there was going to be meat for the Israelites it was going to be God who was going to supply that meat. If there would be a change in their circumstance, God would have to do that. Only God could feed those two million mouths in the wilderness. So in the very beginning we need to learn to look to Jesus and to point other people to Him as well.

I don't know who's relying on you in your life. Maybe it's your spouse. Maybe it's your children. Maybe it's the people at your job who are looking to you to come through for them. That kind of pressure may be more than you can bear. We need to get to the place where we recognize that Jesus and Jesus alone is the one who can make a difference in our lives. We will be like Moses when we worship Him in our own hearts and encourage other people to recognize Him as Lord of Lords and King of Kings and exalt Him in that way in their own lives as well.

In addition to joining in and working with the rest of the body and recognizing that God alone can meet our needs, we need to learn to exercise our faith in God's promise to help us to bear up under the pressure. God is more than able to keep His Word.

Moses said, *"The people whom I am among are 600 thousand men on foot, yet you have said, 'I will give them meat that they may eat for a whole month.' Shall flocks and herds be slaughtered for them to provide enough for them? Or shall all the fish of the sea be gathered together for them to provide enough for them?"* (Num. 11:21-2) There is sarcasm there, like, "What's going to happen, are you going to do a miracle? *"And the Lord said to Moses, 'Has the Lord's arm been shortened? Now you'll see whether what I say will happen to you or not'"* (Num. 11:23)

The Lord Will Bring You Out

I've been in some situations in my life when I couldn't see how we were going to get to the other side and how in the world we were going to get to where God wanted us to be. There are circumstances that are just so overwhelming that it seems like it would take a miracle for us to accomplish or for us to get through the problem, but the question remains, has God's arm been disabled? Has God been so weakened that He cannot act in our lives and in the circumstances that we face? If we're going to make it through and bear up under the pressures of life we need to understand that God is able and we need to exercise faith in God's promises toward us. God's arm has not been shortened. He's able to do what He has promised He would do.

The Lord has promised never to leave us or forsake us. He's promised to make sure that we, His people, will never be begging for bread. He's promised that He's always going to meet our needs no matter what circumstance we find ourselves in. If we will rely on that promise it will relieve the stress and pressure that we encounter.

If God leads you into a task, He's going to see you through to the other side. God is here. The problem is that we don't always see God. We don't always see His hand in our circumstance. We don't always know how He's leading and guiding us. So we lose track of God and end up focusing on how big the problem is.

We've Got His Power Behind Us

It reminds me of the story of Richard Mylander from St. Cloud, Minnesota who was traveling out west. He was in Colorado and being a flatlander from the Midwest he hadn't seen this kind of scenery before in his life. Driving in Colorado, up and down those mountain ranges, he saw a train that was more than a mile long. He came up alongside the train as it was running alongside the highway.

At the back of the train he saw something he'd never seen before. There were two locomotives pushing it. He continued driving beside the train and slowly began to realize how long the train was. He said to himself, "Wow, is that how they do trains out here in these mountain ranges?" When he got to the front of the train, he saw that there were five more engines pulling the train. So there were seven engines in all, five in the front and two more in the back, moving that train through the mountain ranges.

You are sitting in a car on the train of life without realizing how humongous the train is and how difficult it is to pull that train up over one of those mountains. We need to not lose sight of the fact that there are engines, powerful engines, in the front and in the back of our lives, pushing and pulling to get us through. That's the way God works in our lives.

Sometimes we do see the problem and we understand how big it is. We see how long this train is in our lives. We see how well entrenched the train is and we don't understand how this train is going to move over the mountain that exists in our horizon. We can't comprehend how in the world we're going to get to the other side. I want to let you know that God is powerful and He has our back covered and He's out in front before we get there. He is able, more than able, to carry our burdens up over the highest mountain that we find in front of us. It relieves our stress to know that the power of God is operating in our lives.

We can be like the lady who's in the middle car on the train and she just peacefully goes to sleep on her bed. She's not worried about how the train is going to get over the mountain. She can sleep because she has faith in the promise that the engines are going to push and pull that train over and through those towering peaks.

Exercise your faith in God. What a tremendous thing it is to know that God's arm has not been shortened and He is still able. He's a God who is the same yesterday, today, and forever. The same way that He came through miraculously for the Israelites in the wilderness and for the early church and disciples, God can come through miraculously for us today. When we obey Him and when we allow Him to operate in our lives, He's always going to keep His word and the promises He's given to us.

We Must Follow God

Bearing up under pressure also requires obedience to God's direction. We've got to come to the place where we're willing to obey God. Notice in the story that Moses obeyed God. God told him to appoint these 70 elders, so Moses did it. Moses told the people what God said and then he did what God told him to do. He gathered the 70 elders and placed them around the tabernacle the way God told him to do it. They weren't allowed inside but they were allowed around the court.

It is too often that we want God to work in our lives but we don't want to do what God says. We want God's blessings and we want Him to pull us over the hill. We want God to scratch our back and pay the bills. But we don't want to do what God tells us to do. We need to come to the place where we're willing to obey God in every area that He makes it known to us. Some of us have explored every other possibility. We've chased the dollar. We've chased love and we've chased trying to hold our families together. We've chased highs in our lives and we've explored every other possibility. It's time now that we just decide to simply obey God.

I wonder if you are in that situation. You want the blessings of God. You want to bear up under pressure. You want to experience victory in your life. You want to have that abundant life that God has promised. I want to challenge you that the road to that victorious life, and to bear up under the stress in life is to obey God and do what He tells you to do.

Nothing is going to help you stand through the storms of life like obedience to God's Word. When you obey God He leads you and guides you. You don't even always appreciate it. When God leads you, you don't know what would have happened if you took that other job. You don't know what would have happened if you had made that left turn in life. You don't even know what you missed and you don't know what disaster didn't befall you because you obeyed God. You can still, even with all the blessings of God leading you and guiding you, find yourself in a situation where you doubt God and whether His hand is even involved in your life. But you can learn to trust and obey Him and follow His directions.

The Code Is Key

There is a great true story about Hurricane Andrew and a homebuilder in Florida. When the hurricane came through southern Florida, in one neighborhood it blew all the houses away but one. That house stood right in the middle of the neighborhood and it remained standing. When the reporters were going around getting interviews from people they went to the owner of that house and asked him "How is it that your house is standing when the rest of the neighborhood got wiped out by the hurricane? Your house seems as though it hasn't been harmed." The owner's answer was, "Well, I built this house myself and I followed the code. You see if you follow the Boca code, it was written to withstand hurricane winds. All the other houses were built by builders who cut corners and used inferior materials, but I built this house myself and made sure I followed the code."

If you follow God's code in your life and build in obedience to His plan for you life, the storms may blow and the winds may howl but you'll be able to stand for Him. That's the way He intends for it to be, and what He's promised for us. Standing up under pressure requires obedience to God's directions, just as Moses and many other great men of faith have shown us.

After we have joined together with the rest of the body and after we have pointed the attention to Jesus. After we have exercised our faith in God's promises and obeyed God's directions; then we can experience the relief of pressure in our lives. We experience the relief that comes when God performs what He has promised. We experience the relief when God's Spirit enables others to get the job done as we share and delegate part of our burden to other people. We can experience the relief that comes when we watch God gift others to do what we can't because the burden of success or failure was never meant to rest on one member of the body. You can experience the relief that comes when you obey God's word and your building stands in the face of the storm.

Stay For the Long Haul

Stewart Briscoe told a story of how he taught his kids to run when they were young. It was fun then because he could beat his kids. He always came in first and he could run faster and longer than they could. But as his kids grew it got to the point where he didn't enjoy running anymore. He started coming in last. He began huffing and puffing, more and more, and it just wasn't fun anymore.

Then one day his daughter encouraged the whole family to join in a 10,000 metre marathon. That's over 6 miles. It was in Milwaukee and the runners dressed up in all kinds of costumes. Some of the runners were dressed up as beer cans and some as bananas. Some were dressed as different mascots. At the beginning of the race there was nothing but frivolity, fun, joking around, and laughing. The banana was shaking hands with the crowd. It was all fun and games at the beginning of the race.

A mile into the race and the banana and the beer can were hanging over the fence, unable to go any further, out of the race. It got real quiet that second and third mile. Stewart says that people weren't laughing or joking around anymore. It was down to work and the crowd of runners was beginning to thin out. By the time he and his family got to the end of the 6.2 miles the runners were straggling over the finish line and there wasn't much of a crowd waiting for them.

The moral of the story is that at the beginning of any great challenge you can get big crowds of people, goofing around and having fun together. Just as it's an easy thing for us to come into church and say "Amen" and "Hallelujah" and wave our hands and sing praise and worship. That's easy at the beginning of the week, at the start of the race, but that's not the only thing that counts.

God wants us to bear up under pressure. He wants us to bear up under the stress of Monday, Tuesday, Wednesday and Thursday. How many of us still have a smile on our face by the weekend? How many of us are still bearing up under pressure when the week comes to a close. By Friday, when we're punching out, how many of us will still praise God and still be rejoicing in the Lord. If we will obey Him and follow Him and share our burdens with the saints, God will give us the strength to bear up under the pressure and stress and to fight the good fight and to win.

9
Show Me the Ransom

We live in a world where people are bound by all sorts of addictions. There are people bound by alcohol and drugs. There are people bound by cigarettes, pornography, illicit relationships, out-of-control bad tempers and many other sins. There are some things that we don't even consider sins but they bind people just the same. There are people bound by everything from endless hours watching soap operas to overeating and compulsive shopping. If we stop and think about it all of us are prone to bondage by a number of things. Jesus Christ came to set us free and we need to experience the freedom He has available for each one of us.

God Makes The Provision

There is a phrase made popular by a movie that says, "Show me the money." But God says, "Show Me the Ransom". The idea of paying for redemption, and the ransom God paid for our redemption, is critical throughout the Bible. When God was giving Moses the law at Mt. Sinai, He said, *"And in all the land of your possession, you shall grant redemption of the land. If one of your brethren becomes poor and has sold some of his possessions and if his redeeming relative comes to redeem it, then he may redeem what his brother sold. Or if the man has no one to redeem it, but he himself becomes able to redeem it then let him count the years since its sale and restore the remainder to the man to whom he sold it that he may return it to his possession"* (Lev. 25:24-27). In other words, God is saying that if you can't redeem it, I'm going to make provision so somebody else, a kinsman, someone in your family, is able to redeem it for you. If it becomes possible for you to make redemption and restore what was lost, whether it was in a debt conflict, sold to get you out of prison, or transferred to buy back one of your kids, there is a provision to pay a ransom to get that possession.

Redemption Is Always Possible

The first thing to understand is that God makes sure that redemption is always possible, regardless of what your circumstance might be and regardless of the sin that has grabbed hold of you. Whatever prisons you might find yourself in, God makes sure that freedom is possible. He makes it possible for you to have victory in any circumstance. It's necessary that He provide the ransom because we can't do for ourselves.

There is a Reader's Digest story about a 90-year-old man named Harvey Pinnick, who in his early years in the 1920s bought a little red spiral book. He loved to play golf and started writing down all his observations and all the things he learned throughout the years about playing the game of golf. He called it his little red book. When he was much older the only man he had ever shown it to was his brother. His brother referred him to a writer who looked at the book and told him he should get it published. Harvey asked, "Do you really think this is worth publishing?" The writer said, "Oh yeah." And he took the book and presented it to a couple of publishers.

A few days later the writer called back and since Harvey wasn't home he left a message with Harvey's wife that went something like this, "I have a publisher who has agreed to an advance of $90,000." A couple of days later the writer friend came and met Harvey. He was puzzled by the forlorn look on Harvey's face. Harvey was sort of distraught. Harvey told the writer, "You know, as much as I would like to have this book published, there's no way with all my medical bills and my finances the way they are that I can come up with a $90,000 advance." Harvey was ready to pull the book back when the writer explained, "No, Harvey, you don't have to come up with the $90,000. They give the money to you."

The expression Harvey must have had on his face is the expression we should have when we understand that God has paid the ransom for us. We don't have to try to come up with it (as if we could), because He makes sure that the ransom is always available. It doesn't matter what your bank account adds up to. It doesn't matter what your station in life might be or what socio-economic group you might belong to, God makes sure that a ransom is available. So when sin says, "Show me the ransom", God doesn't leave you in the lurch. He makes sure that it is available.

A People Set Apart

This same principle is discussed in Numbers Chapter 3. The ransom for a man had to be another man. This is one of those chapters where you can get lost in all the listing of names, jobs, and other things that are in there. But you can get a sense of what God is saying by looking at the 6th verse in this chapter. The Lord is speaking to Moses and says to him, *"Bring the tribe of Levi near. And present them before me, Aaron the priest, that they may serve him."* In previous chapters in Numbers, Moses was told to take a census and to count all the people. He was told to count all the Israelites except for one tribe, the Levites. God wanted to count the men who could go to war but He had a different plan for the Levites.

So after counting and arranging all the other tribes and telling them how they were going to pitch their tents and march through the wilderness, God gave instructions to bring the Levites to Him and cause them to draw near, that they may serve Him. He says, *"Now behold, I myself have taken the Levites from among the children of Israel, instead of every firstborn who opens the womb among the children of Israel, therefore the Levites shall be mine"* (Num. 3:12). He is saying, "Bring the Levites here because the job I have for them is to be the ransom for all the first born in Israel that were freed in the land of Egypt."

Remember when the Israelites were in Egypt and the death angel passed over? Only the houses that had blood on the doorposts when the death angel passed over were spared their firstborn. In every other house the firstborn died. God is saying that since I've spared the first, I've freed all the people from that plague, but I need a ransom. Show me the ransom. The ransom in this case was the whole tribe of Levi. God said, *"Because all the first born are Mine, on the day which I struck all the firstborn in the land of Egypt, I sanctified to Myself all the first born of Israel, both man and beast, they shall be Mine, I am the Lord"* (Num. 3:13). And when God says, *"I am the Lord,"* that's it. That's a firm "Amen." The Levites were His, He claimed them and that was the ransom He demanded.

A Life For a Life

Now God divided all the sons of Levi by families and they were in the service of the Lord and the Tabernacle. There was the family of Gershon, the family of Kohath, the family of Mirari, and He gave each of the families of Levi a particular job to do. You can read through all the families and the various jobs that God had given them to do in Numbers 3.

For example, Gershon had care of the tabernacle of meeting, which included the tent with all its coverings. Each family had an area of responsibility in which they were supposed to serve. *"All who were numbered of the Levites whom Moses and Aaron numbered at the commandment of the Lord by their families. All the males, a month old and above were twenty-two thousand (22,000)"* (Num. 3:39). That's a number you can just run over if you're reading too quickly.

A few verses later God says, *"And you shall take the Levites from me, I am the Lord, instead of all the first born from among the children of Israel, and the livestock of the Levites, instead of all the firstborn among the livestock, of the children of Israel"* (Num. 3:41). In other words, this swap is where He's going to take the Levites in exchange for the firstborn. There were 22,000 Levites in exchange for the firstborn males according to the number of names from a month old and above. Of those who were numbered there were 22,273. (Num.3:43). This is very close in number to the 22,000 Levites with a difference of only 273.

Was it just by coincidence that these numbers were so close? The principle established here is that the ransom for a man has to be another man. The proper exchange that God wants to establish for your ransom and for my ransom has to be another life. If you are going to be set free from the sin that so easily besets you, from the judgement of God against your sin, from Satan's claims on your life, God says, "Show me the ransom". And that ransom is a life for a life.

God even had a plan for the extra 273. He didn't want us to get the impression that they were just going to skip in without having to deal with the ransom principle. When you look toward the end of the chapter, you'll notice that He allowed, by His grace, for these 273 to still experience the freedom and the blessings of God for some shekels they had in their pockets. *"For the redemption of the 273 of the first born of the children of Israel who are more than the number of Levites, you take five shekels for each one individually"* (Num. 3:46). It was an amount they could come up with and they brought that money to Aaron and Moses for the work of the Tabernacle.

In 1 Corinthians 10, we understand that the things that we see in the Old Testament were given for us today. We should learn what the symbolism means so we can learn from the experience of the people in the Old Testament. From this seemingly boring piece of history God wants us to learn that He takes the ransom principle very seriously.

God Does Not Wink At Sin

You might think that God is this wonderful, forgiving, loving God up in heaven, just waiting to forgive you of all of your sins and your shortcomings. You might feel that God is the kind of God who knows that you are unable to do the things you are supposed to do so He'll just cut you some slack and let you slide on all those areas that you fall short. The reality is that God is a holy and righteous God and He does not wink at your sin. He sits on His throne in all His holiness and righteousness and says, "Show me the ransom." That's what He wants. He's not playing games.

You can't say "OK, but how about half today and half on Tuesday." And God doesn't accept American Express. He doesn't accept personal checques. Some people think they can write a checque and drop it in the offering or send it to starving children in Ethiopia and that's going to satisfy God. But

God says show me the ransom and the only ransom that makes sense to Him, that will satisfy His just demands against our sin, is a man for a man. That leaves us in a very, very tight situation. That leaves us in a situation where we are unable to supply what God requires.

Here is what you should know about this redemption. The idea behind the word that is translated "redemption" in Numbers 3:12-13 is deliverance. The whole purpose for a ransom was to pay for your freedom and for your deliverance. What people don't seem to understand is that before you came to Christ and before you entered into an agreement for Him to be your ransom, you were bound in the prison of sin. Satan had you shackled.

We can have deliverance from the many addictions and various things that are out there tying up and destroying lives. We can have freedom from all that. He whom the Son sets free is free indeed. We should be happy that the ransom has been supplied because that redemption, that ransom means freedom for us. It means deliverance for us. It means victory for us, no matter what the circumstance might be in our lives.

Before you can experience that kind of freedom, God says show me the ransom. You can't break out from the prison of your temper by yourself. You can't break out from the prison of overeating or illicit relationships or compulsive action by yourself. God supplies all that you need to have a victorious life, a life of freedom from the sin that so easily besets you. The price is paid by the ransom of Jesus Christ on the Cross.

You Can't Pay The Ransom

The other aspect of this ransom principle is that the redemption of a soul costs more than you can come up with. That principle of a life for a life means that you have to give your life in order to experience that kind of freedom. On the outset that principle doesn't seem to make sense. If you lose your life then you don't have a life. It's more than you can come up with to satisfy God's demand against your sin. But I thank God that when we ran out of something to offer Him, Psalm 111:9 says God sent the ransom price, a price that is more than we can come up with on our own.

Let me share a story about a father back in the horse and buggy days. He had gone to school one afternoon to pick up his three kids, a 9, 11, and 17-year-old. He pulled up to the school house and hopped out of the horse carriage and his kids jumped in. Before he could climb back up onto the carriage something startled the horses and they took off running with his three kids inside the carriage until they were out of sight.

He gathered a search party and they looked all night for the carriage and the kids. It was winter time so it was cold and snowy. It wasn't until the next day that they found the kids. The 17-year-old was sobbing and crying over the frozen dead bodies of her younger brother and sister. The father reached out and began to hug her as she sobbed. After she regained a little bit of her composure she turned to her father and said, "I tried to keep them warm. I took off my coat and tried to wrap them up but my coat wasn't big enough to get all the way around both of them and they froze to death."

It grabs at your heart when your coat isn't big enough to solve your problems. It's terribly frustrating to find that in spite of all the righteousness you try to muster, that your coat of personal righteousness and wisdom is just not big enough to solve the issues that you bring to the table. I'm happy to know that God's coat of righteousness supplied by Jesus Christ is big enough to wrap around all of our problems. It is big enough to wrap around all of our bondage to sin.

No matter what the issue or terrible circumstance in your life, no matter what the problem you face might be, the ransom of Jesus, His coat, is big enough to meet God's requirements and set you free. What a wonderful thing. The blood that Jesus Christ shed on the Cross is enough to cover all of our sins, all of our lusting, all of our lying, all of our cheating, all of our hatred, all of our faults. Our sins are covered by this wonderful atonement from His blood being shed for us.

His Coat Is Big Enough For All

One of the things about the ransom payment of the blood of Jesus is that nobody is going to be able to stand before God one day and say, "The guy right in front of me in line used up the last drop of blood and there wasn't enough blood for me." None of us are going to have to worry about being a day late and a dollar short when we face the Lord. Everyone who receives Jesus Christ by faith, everybody who gets in that gospel line having received Him as their personal Lord and Saviour is going to be met with a coat of righteousness big enough to wrap around them. It's a coat big enough to cover all our scars. It's big enough and wonderful enough to make us completely acceptable to our Lord and Saviour, Jesus Christ.

Through Jesus Christ we are given all the righteousness we need to satisfy God's demand against us. I'm not afraid when God says, "Tony, show me the ransom!" I'm not worried that He tells me to put up or shut up. Why? Because He has supplied the ransom of Himself, a man for a man. The God-man Jesus Christ left the heights of heaven and came down to this sin-cursed earth and made Himself a ransom for me. He paid the price I needed to pay. So I say to the Lord, "I thank you and I praise and worship You for what You have done for me."

Live Like You Are Redeemed

Sometimes we think that messages about redemption are for a Gospel crusade. That it is for the guy who doesn't know Jesus Christ, for the unsaved out there in the world. We think to ourselves, "I already have a handle on all that. Why do I need to get up early in the morning to make it to church by 8, just to hear the pastor talk about redemption. I don't need to hear that all over again." But the story of redemption and the principle of redemption needs to be rehearsed by believers because when we really know what we have, we will live differently, not just once, but daily. It will change the way we go through life.

First of all, we need to live in the realization that our deliverance is bought and paid for. From the time we wake up on Monday morning to the moment we fall asleep on Sunday night we need to live in the understanding that our deliverance has already been accomplished. The work is finished.

Christians are some of the prime candidates for carrying around guilt complexes. We drag our old sins around like a huge sack of potatoes that just weighs us down. Christians are some of the worst people when it comes to understanding that God has taken care of all that. We need to live our lives in the realization that while God demands payment for our sins, the payment has been made. The ransom has been put on the table.

We can also live our lives in the full realization that we don't have to be fearful about our relationship with God. We don't have to be timid about approaching God. We are accepted by Him. We can jump on His lap and wrap our arms around His neck. We can call Him Abba, Father, Daddy! We can enjoy a wonderful relationship with Him. Not a fearful relationship but an intimate and worshipful relationship with Him. Why? Because we have that full realization that all His demands against our sin have been paid.

We Have His Resources

Just because He made the payment doesn't mean that we come to God with some kind of delusion about our sin. It doesn't mean we should feel that we have no sin. It means that we approach God with the full realization that we fall short and there is sin that has to be dealt with in our lives, but at the same time thanking God that the price has been paid and we don't have to carry that load around with us. Satan can't bind us and the flesh doesn't have to win anymore. We have the victory because the price has been paid.

Not only do we need the realization that our deliverance is bought and paid for, we need to stop digging into our own pockets for the resources needed for that deliverance. We have a wonderful resource in the blood of Jesus Christ, yet many Christians don't take advantage of that resource. They fight life with their own resources and many times they lose.

Imagine this. You're in a financial strait so you look up Donald Trump in the phone book. You happen to see his name and phone number so you make a call to Donald and his secretary actually puts you through. You're on the line with Donald Trump and you ask him if you can make an appointment, telling him, "I have some financial problems. Can I please come in and see you?" He says, "Oh sure, come on in, I have plenty of time next Tuesday morning."

So on Tuesday you walk into his office and you lay your financial situation on the table before him. You say, "Donald, my finances are just in a mess. I need a major infusion of cash to put me back on the right track. Just imagine that Donald Trump pulls out his ATM card and says "My heart goes out to you, here's my ATM card." He hands it to you and says, "I'm going to need it by Thursday but take it and go solve your problems. Come back on Thursday and let me know how you made out."

Can you imagine if you were walking around with Donald Trump's ATM card in your back pocket, yet you continued haggling and arguing with your creditors? You're still thinking about your paycheque two weeks from Friday and still trying to negotiate terms with your creditors while you're carrying around Donald Trumps ATM card with unlimited resources at your fingertips.

And that's the way it is for a lot of Christians. We have God's unlimited resources provided to us in the blood of Jesus. We've got a claim to certain and eternal victory, yet we're walking around negotiating with the devil. We go through life listening to his terms and his conditions, frustrated by the circumstances that we find ourselves in. It's high time that we stop listening to the devil. It's time for us to stop negotiating with him. It's time that we decide to reach into the resources that God has provided through His finished work, the ransom of Christ on the Cross. We can take out His Glory card and use it.

You've Got To Know How To Use The Card

If you have Donald Trump's ATM card in your pocket and you put it in the machine there are a few numbers called pin numbers that you had better know. The card without those few key numbers isn't going to do you a whole lot of good. In the same way, the blood of Jesus Christ is a wonderful resource but there are some key pin numbers that you've got to have a handle on. There are some instructions that you've got to follow in order to use those riches in Glory.

Christians are sometimes frustrated because they understand that our heavenly Father has the resources. They know they have the Glory Card, they just don't know how to use it.

They can't tap into the account because they don't know how to approach God. They stand at the ATM, frustrated about how to access all the stuff they see in His word.

As Christians, we don't just need more worship. We don't just need more praise and more music and we don't just need more emotion. We also need to do some serious Bible study. We need to do some hard work. We need to do some digging so we can find the pin numbers that give us access to the resources that God has for us. You can jump around on Sunday morning but that's not going to help you on Tuesday night if you don't know how to access what God has for you. The challenge for us is that we need to stop digging into our own pockets and get into His Word and understand how to access all that He has provided for us.

Live In The Victory

When God says, "Show me the ransom", we can say there's no problem because Jesus Christ has provided the ransom for us. Even if no one else joins in we should be praising God today because He has paid the price for our sin. The victory is ours and we can live in that understanding. Our freedom has been secured. Satan can shut up and sit down. There is no bondage that can bind us, no sin that can defeat us.

When I sin big time all I need to do is confess it to Him. If we will only approach Him with a sincere heart, He's willing to forgive us our sin and cleanse us from all unrighteousness and that's a wonderful thing. Thank God that His coat of righteousness is big enough to get all the way around us. We must praise God and worship Him because of all that He has done for us, for who He is and how He has exchanged His life for ours and enabled us to experience and walk in freedom.

10
Spy for What

Anyone who has sat under my preaching for any length of time knows I like to relate things to sports. One of the things a quarterback has to be able to do is read the defense. It helps him to appreciate where he should go with the ball and what his next move should be. As he approaches the line of scrimmage he spies out the defense and checks to see where every body is and what everybody is up to. Then he can audible, make his corrections, and deliver his pass at the right spot and at the right time.

It's very similar with missionaries. When missionaries move into a foreign country and into an unknown culture to do ministry, they have to take some time to interpret the culture. They have to get to know the lay of the land. They have to figure out who is with them and who is against them. And they have to figure out what all the aspects of that culture mean before they can do effective ministry.

God Sends in Advance

In Numbers 13:2, the Lord tells Moses, *"Send men to spy out the land of Canaan."* This is the land God had promised to the nation of Israel. He told them to check it out, to find out where things were and where the enemy was. He wanted them to find out what was for them, what was against them, and what were going to be the hindrances to them occupying that land. Throughout the chapter you find there are many things that God tells them to look for.

The question that arises for us is, "Spy for what?" What are we supposed to look for as we spy out our lives, our circumstances, the promises of God, and the lay of the land He has situated each of us in? What are we supposed to be watching? As we look at what God told the spies to look for in the land of Canaan, it will help us to know what we should look for in our own lives and circumstances.

What Kind of Land is it?

The first thing the spies were to look for was to see if the land was good or bad. It's a very interesting question. What does God mean by 'good' or 'bad'? I believe God was trying to get the Israelites to make a value judgement on His promises. God told them that the land was going to be a land flowing with milk and honey and that it was going to be a wonderful land they could call home. He had painted a beautiful picture of the land they had traveled to for so many years and through so many hardships. God knew that the land was good, but He wanted them to go and see for themselves and make their own value judgement.

In the very same way God has made us some promises today. He has promised us an abundant life. He has promised us that He would go with us as we sing in praise and worship. He's that Good Shepherd who will lead us into the valley of the shadow of death. He's promised never to leave us or forsake us. He's promised that you will never see His seed forsaken or begging bread. God has told us in the book that we have these promises but still He tells us to spy them out to see if they are good or bad. God knows that the promises are good but He also knows that until you taste and see for yourself, until you experience them yourself, you don't really know.

The worship leader at our 8 o'clock service made the comment before the offering that some of us need to test God and see whether or not we can out-give God in our offering. That's one way of spying it out. Some of us know in our heads that we can't out-give God because it's written in the Book, but we've never spied it out for ourselves. We've never tested it. It's just head knowledge until you really put it into practice and stand on the promises. Until you walk into that land yourself and take a look at it you really don't know.

It's one thing to sit in Sunday school and have your teacher tell you that God's Word is 'Yes' and 'Amen'. It's one thing to have the preacher in church tell you that you can trust God with all the decisions that you have in your life and with all the situations that you face. But it's a whole different ball game on Monday when you're making the decisions or on Thursday when the struggle is right up against you and you've got to either make a right turn or left turn. It's a different ballgame when you're about to be laid off and God is saying to trust me and go over there when you think that the safety net is over here. So spy out the land, check it out for yourselves, and make a value judgement whether or not God's promises are good or bad.

How Wealthy is the Land?

Further on in Numbers Chapter 13, God says to go look and see if the land is rich or poor. *"And how is the land, is it fat or lean?"* (Num. 13:20a). The question before these Israelites was simply to discover if what God had promised would sustain them. Would what God promised meet their needs? Would He run out of resources halfway through? In your life, is God going to leave you hanging? Is God going to promise you the world and have you out on a string and then cut the string and say, "I just ran out of money and resources and what you need and I can't help you anymore." It doesn't make any sense going on the promises of God if you're only going to have an abundant life for a day or a month because God comes up short and His 'Master' Card gets spit back at you.

I thank God that we serve a King who owns houses and land and the cattle on a thousand hills. Somebody once said that when God is finished with the cattle He owns the hills too! We worship a rich God, a God who never runs short, a God who can always meet your need and a God who is never going to leave you hanging. When you spy out God's promises and walk down a few of those trails and trials with God, you come to realize that He's always got more for you and He never runs short.

Even after all the promises, we still question in our hearts if this life that God has promised us really is abundant, or just talk? Are we here raising our hands and singing our songs just as an exercise or is there some reality behind it? Can we really depend on God's resources when we don't know where our next meal is coming from or the next tank of gas for the car, or the next month's rent? God tells us to keep on going on and continue pushing forward. You need to know that God is rich and is always going to be there to meet your need. Someone might not hand you a minivan. Someone might not meet that need the way that you have been praying for. Someone might not drop a $10 bill in your pocket when your pockets are empty, but somehow God is going to make sure that His people get taken care of. Is the land rich or poor? You better check it out. Don't go too much further down the Christian pathway if you're not sure about what you're stepping into.

The Forests in Our Lives

As we read further in the chapter, God tells the Israelites to look and see if there are forests in the land. (Num. 13:20). The first time I read that I said, "Why would God tell them to look and see if there are forests? What does that have to do with anything?" But then I realized, that's where the enemy would hide so you couldn't see them. The forests would be one of the dangerous places that you would have to account for in your lay of the land. So God told the Israelites to send spies and to check out the locations of the forests. There are forests in the landscape of your life. There are places where the enemy is hanging out, ready to pounce. He's lurking there, seeking whom he can devour.

There are places in your life that you know are dangerous for you. For some people, one place might be dangerous and another not. For somebody else it might be the other way around. You better know where the forests are in your life and know the friends that drag you down. Know where those places are that mess up your walk with Christ and where the enemy is hanging out. Those are the dangerous places that you need to stay away from. We need to be like the quarterback, checking out the defense and knowing where the enemy is so he won't fall prey to their trap.

Don't be naive and think that you are not going to be involved in a struggle. If you name the Name, put the tag on your chest and say, "I'm a Christian", and you begin to walk with the Lord, there's going to be an enemy and a fight. There's going to be warfare. So don't be naïve. Spy out the land. Have things accounted for so you can be ready to fight for God and for your very soul.

Size Up the People

God also says to see whether the people are strong or weak. (Num. 13:18). God knew that they would be up against some giants in the land. The enemy was strong. At the end of the chapter some of the spies reported back to Moses, *"There we saw the giants, the descendants of Anak, and we were like grasshoppers in our sight compared to them. And we were like grasshoppers in their sight as they looked to us"* (Num. 13:20). The word 'giants' used here is the same word *"Nephilim"* used in Genesis, chapter 6. We're not really sure of the best translation for this word. King James and most of the English Bibles use the word giants because it's the closest translation that we can come up with for that word. In some secular writings that use that Hebrew word, the meaning is not physiological anomalies standing 20 feet high, but rather very powerful men.

A king, during that time, built his house up on top of a hill and he would have serfs to cultivate the land around. The serfs would provide food, goods, and services for the king and the king in turn, being a mighty warrior and the leader of mighty warriors, would provide protection for the people who lived in the communities around him and allow them to till the land and grow crops. These powerful warriors were sometimes called Nephilim and they were the enemy that would fight against Israel when they came to occupy the land.

These spies found that the land was filled with these powerful warriors and great kings, descendents from Anak. We're not sure who Anak is but he was probably a real powerful guy who gave a lot of land to his sons. God knew He was able to give the Israelites the victory but He wanted His people to appreciate the fact that this battle was way over their heads.

God Fights Our Battles

If God hadn't commanded Moses to send spies into Canaan to check out the land for themselves and to report back about the giants, the people would have never known what a great feat it was that God went before them and helped them to wipe out the enemy. They may have been tempted to take the credit for themselves and say, "Hey, check out what we did! We just marched into this land and took over! We're bad! We are some terrible warriors!" But God before they set foot into the land and before any fighting started, He wanted them to appreciate that there was no way that they, in their own strength, could conquer the enemy. Without Him they were way over their heads.

God Wants Us to Depend on Him

Sometimes God wants you and me to look at the situations that we face in our family, our finances, our health, and to come to the conclusion, "This is way over my head. I can't even lift a finger to this problem. I'm like a grasshopper compared to this situation. Lord, I've done all that I can do. I've pulled my hair out. I've cried all my tears. I've stayed up nights until I can't stay up anymore." And when we come to that place and we know there is nothing we can do, God says "Now I've got you right where I want you. Now I can do something for you because you will recognize when I give you the victory that it was Me and not you. You didn't have a thing to do with it. It was My power and not yours." What a wonderful lesson for Israel and it's one that we can apply to our own life. We need to spy out our land, face the enemy and know that God will win the battle.

God At Work

Gladys Alward, a missionary to China in the middle of the 20th century, took care of about 100 orphans. China was having a revolution and the people were trying to flee into the free part of China. She decided that she wasn't going to leave without the orphans, so, with only one assistant, she gathered up the 100 children and tried to make it to free China on the other side of the mountain ranges, even though she had no idea how she was going to do it. One night she stayed up all night in despair because she kept thinking there was no way in the world they could make it. There was just no way.

It was on one of these nights that a 13-year-old orphan went to her and said, "Gladys, don't be so in despair. Remember how God led Moses and the Israelites across the Red Sea? Remember how Moses put out the staff and the waters parted and they were able to get across." Gladys' responded, "Well, I'm not Moses. God did that for Moses but what is He going to do for me?" And the 13 year-old girl responded, "Yeah, you're not Moses. But God is still God."

God is not asking you to be Moses. He's not asking you to be a super hero. He's not asking you to spin out of a phone booth with a big "S" on your chest. You don't have to be faster than a speeding bullet or to leap tall buildings with a single bound. He's simply asking you to trust Him. God is asking you to spy out the situation, get an accurate appraisal of what's going on, realize that there are giants in the land, realize that you can't win it on your own, then come to Him and trust Him and recognize that He's still God and He's stronger than the strongest enemy out there. Spy out the land and then appreciate His victory when it comes.

Look for the Enemy

But there is another aspect of spying out the land. Numbers 13:18 says, *"See whether the people are few or many."* What difference could it make if the people are few or many? God had promised them the victory. It didn't matter whether there were thousands of mighty warriors fighting against the Israelites or just a handful. But God wanted them to see how many there were and He wouldn't give them the victory until they understood that they were up against a number and an obstacle too great for them to handle. Otherwise they would never appreciate it. God empowered them only after they understood that it was impossible.

In our lives today the enemy takes many forms but He is out there. He is on your job, in your home, in your neighborhood, and certainly on your TV, the internet, the radio, and in magazines and newspapers. We don't have to spy very long to figure out that the enemy is many. God wants us to know where he is and that he is plentiful.

God Wants You Involved

I don't know where the idea comes from that all a Christian needs to do is just lie back in bed, watch the TV, and let God give them the victory. God doesn't want you waiting on Him to give you the victory. After you've spied out the land and seen that the giants are many, He wants you to strategize. With His help you will come up with a plan and know how to proceed and it will be a plan God can give you the power to carry out.

Then He wants you to take action. He wants you going somewhere and doing something. He will be with you and give you the victory as you proceed against the enemy. You don't have to spy very long in your life to see that the enemy is all over the place and you don't need to be discouraged or paranoid about it. The Creator of the universe is with you.

Check Out the Environment

In Numbers 13:19, God says, *"Go look and see whether you are up against camps or strongholds."* The camps were simply a group of tents where people lived. They were temporary housing and you could run over a pup tent a whole lot easier than you could run over a stronghold. The strongholds were made up of four to five cities surrounded by walls with soldiers on top and strong moats around the thick walls. You couldn't just run them over. It required a different strategy to attack a stronghold as opposed to attacking a tent. So God told them to spy out the land and see if they were up against pup tents or strongholds.

When the spies came back the conclusion was that there were strongholds all over the land. It wasn't going to be just a matter of knocking down and running through somebody's campsite. The big, fortified walls would have to come down.

The encouraging message for us is that we don't have to be discouraged even when we're up against strongholds. There are situations in your life that seem as if they just won't budge. You're not making any progress. You're pushing with all your might and you're hitting your head up against a brick wall. That's a stronghold in your life. People fight strongholds of every kind, including addictions, bad tempers and bad attitudes. We can be encouraged even when we go against those strongholds. Some situations in your life are like facing a pup tent. You say a prayer, God answers and it's done. You move onto the next issue. But there are other issues that you've been praying for and crying about and that have been on the prayer list for years, year after year, and they don't seem to be moving. Those are strongholds in your life.

Victory in Christ

You don't have to be discouraged because God promises us the victory. His promises are still rich and not poor. He is still stronger than the most powerful enemy or the greatest stronghold. Before you go any further with Jesus, you need to be encouraged about the fact that He is stronger than anything you come up against. As a believer in Jesus Christ we don't have to be paranoid about the enemy. We might see the enemy in the forest or around the next corner, but that doesn't need to make a believer paranoid.

I'm not worried about where the devil is hiding. That doesn't concern me **because greater is He that is in me than he that is in the world** (1 John 4:4). We can stroll down the trail with God on our side, not being paranoid about all the positions that the enemy holds because the devil is just a liar. He really has no hold on us. For the child of God, he's a lion with a big roar and no bite. The further you walk with Jesus the more the enemy might fight back. The more he might roar in your ear. But the further you walk with Jesus, the less the enemy will concern you. You've got the assurance of victory on your side.

Get an Understanding of God's Power

Bringing it back to sports for the guys, Roger Clemens was a big league pitcher and in 1986 he was playing his second year. He was in his first all-star game in his second season in the American league. During the regular season games he never had to bat because the American league has a designated hitter so the pitchers don't have to go to bat. So here he is in his first all-star game and he has to go up to bat for the first time. He looks up and guess who's on the pitcher's mound? It was Dwight Gooden standing there in the prime of his career. He had just won the Cy Young Award.

So the first fastball comes down the pike and Roger looks at the ball as it goes 'swoosh', right by him. It scared him a little bit. He stepped out of the box, looked at Gary Carter, the catcher, and said, "Is that what my fastball looks like?" And Gary Carter says, "You bet it does." Roger gets back in the batter's box but he's scared at the speed of the ball. It's just a frightening thing to stand up against such a fast pitch. Eventually, Dwight struck him out.

Clemens went back to the pitcher's mound, but after seeing how intimidating a major league fastball is and how hard it is to hit, he understood the power he had in his hands with that little ball. He went back on the mound and threw three perfect innings. Why? It was because he had renewed confidence about the power in his hands. He had spied it out for himself and he had a real appreciation for his ability with a baseball.

We, as Christians, need a renewed appreciation for the power that we have in our hands with Christ Jesus. We need to understand the resources that are available to us. It's not until we step into the batter's box, until we spy out the land for ourselves that we will see God solve our problems. It's not until we see God's hand in our lives and God acting in your circumstances that we appreciate our wonderful Saviour. We have this wonderful God who's there to back us up when we do His will.

I like the words in the song, "We're marching to Zion, beautiful, beautiful Zion." Let those who don't know our God refuse to sing. But those of us who know our God, those of us who have Him walking by our side, those of us who know what it is to have the power of God in us and the power of the Word of God in our lives, let us sing praises to God. Let us worship Him. And let us never be afraid of what the enemy has to say. Let's spy out the land and be ready to conquer.

Invitation

I want to challenge you that winning in this life starts with a meaningful relationship with God. It starts first of all by coming to Christ and asking Him into your life. Maybe you are not sure that Jesus is in your life, not sure that He's forgiven you of your sins and that if you died today you're on your way to heaven. Maybe you think so, maybe you hope so, maybe you're doing the best you can, but if you're not absolutely sure that your sins are forgiven and that you're right with God, you can be sure, right now, by saying this prayer to God.

A Salvation Prayer

Dear Jesus, thank You for making me and loving me, even when I've ignored You and went my own way. I realize I need You in my life and I'm sorry for my sins, I ask You to forgive me. Thank You for dying on the cross for me. Please help me to understand it more. As much as I know how, I want to follow You from now on. Please come into my life and make me new a person inside. I accept Your gift of salvation. Please help me to grow now as a Christian.

I trust that you'll take advantage of this opportunity to get right with God. He says if you'll come to Him, "He will in no wise cast you out." If you ask Him to forgive you, He'll forgive you. If you confess your sins to Him, "He will forgive your sins and cleanse you from all unrighteousness," past, present and future. He'll confirm in you that you are a child of the King. He'll not only adopt you, but you'll be born into His family, as well. Once you are in the family, as Jesus says, no one can snatch you out of His hand. No one can mess with you anymore and you can't even wriggle out of His fist-lock yourself. That's the kind of powerful, loving and forever victory He is offering you today.